From Work to Wealth: A Roadmap to Retirement Success

Matthew Lang
Wealth Shield Financial

Copyright © 2024 by Matthew Lang and Advisors Excel, LLC.
All rights reserved. No part of this publication may be reproduced, distributed, or transmitted in any form or by any means, including photocopying, recording, or other electronic or mechanical methods, without the prior written permission of the publisher, except in the case of brief quotations embodied in critical reviews and certain other noncommercial uses permitted by copyright law. For permission requests, write to the publisher at the address below. These materials are provided to you by Matthew Lang for informational purposes only and Matthew Lang and Advisors Excel, LLC expressly disclaim any and all liability arising out of or relating to your use of same. The provision of these materials does not constitute legal or investment advice and does not establish an attorney-client relationship between you and Matthew Lang. No tax advice is contained in these materials. You are solely responsible for ensuring the accuracy and completeness of all materials as well as the compliance, validity, and enforceability of all materials under any applicable law. The advice and strategies found within may not be suitable for every situation. You are expressly advised to consult with a qualified attorney or other professional in making any such determination and to determine your legal or financial needs. No warranty of any kind, implied, expressed, or statutory, including but not limited to the warranties of title and non-infringement of third-party rights, is given with respect to this publication.

Matthew Lang/Wealth Shield Financial LLC
45 River Road, Suite 3
Summit, NJ 07901
https://wealthshieldfinancial.com/

Book layout ©2022 Advisors Excel, LLC

From Work to Wealth: A Roadmap to Retirement Success/Wealth Shield Financial.

ISBN 9798321730829

Matthew Lang is registered as a Registered Representative and is a licensed insurance agent in the states of California, Connecticut, Florida, Indiana, Kansas, Michigan, North Carolina, New Jersey, New York, Ohio, Pennsylvania, South Carolina, Texas (#1802675), and Virginia.

Wealth Shield Financial, LLC is an independent financial services firm that helps individuals create retirement strategies using a variety of investment and insurance products to custom suit their needs and objectives. Securities offered through Madison Avenue Securities, LLC (MAS), member FINRA/SIPC. Wealth Shield Financial LLC and MAS are not affiliated companies.

The contents of this book are provided for informational purposes only and are not intended to serve as the basis for any financial decisions. Any tax, legal, or estate planning information is general in nature. Please remember that converting an employer plan account to a Roth IRA is a taxable event. Increased taxable income from the Roth IRA conversion may have several consequences. Be sure to consult with a qualified tax advisor before making any decisions regarding your IRA. It should not be construed as legal or tax advice. Always consult an attorney or tax professional regarding the applicability of this information to your unique situation.

Information presented is believed to be factual and up-to-date, but we do not guarantee its accuracy, and it should not be regarded as a complete analysis of the subjects discussed. All expressions of opinion are those of the author as of the date of publication and are subject to change. Content should not be construed as personalized investment advice nor should it be interpreted as an offer to buy or sell any securities mentioned. A financial advisor should be consulted before implementing any of the strategies presented.

Investing involves risk, including the potential loss of principal. No investment strategy can guarantee a profit or protect against loss in periods of declining values. Any references to protection benefits or guaranteed/lifetime income streams refer only to fixed insurance products, not securities or investment products. Insurance and annuity product guarantees are backed by the financial strength and claims-paying ability of the issuing insurance company. Wealth Shield Financial, LLC is not affiliated with the U.S. government or any governmental agency.

Any names used in the examples in this book are hypothetical only and do not represent actual clients.

"If you fail to plan, you are planning to fail!"

~ Benjamin Franklin

"Rule number one is never lose money. Rule number two is never forget rule number one."

~ Warren Buffet

"When everything seems to be going against you, remember that an airplane takes off against the wind, not with it."

~ Henry Ford

To my father for encouraging me to join this industry twenty-one years ago. Also, to my wife and children, who are always supporting me as a financial advisor, a small business owner, and most importantly, a husband and father.

Table of Contents

The Importance of Planning i
Longevity 1
Taxes 21
Market Volatility 33
Retirement Income 43
Social Security 61
401(k)s, IRAs, and Roth IRAs 77
Annuities 89
Estate and Legacy Planning Strategies 99
Women Retire Too 109
Indexed Universal Life Insurance 123
Long-Term Care Insurance 133
Finding a Financial Professional 139
Acknowledgments 147
About the Author 149

PREFACE
The Importance of Planning

Many families fail to plan, and there are horror stories everywhere. In my practice at Wealth Shield Financial, we help stave off catastrophes by meeting spouses and individuals when they're pre-retirees and still have time to plan. Early intervention is key to preventing missteps that incur loss of wealth. We guide all our clients through a detailed yet systematic planning process so that they never find themselves in difficult circumstances.

There are many people who think that if they save enough, there's no need to plan. Plenty of people amass a fortune. They're often diligent savers. They've spent their whole life guarding their money. That's great, but unfortunately, it doesn't guarantee you'll have the quality of life you desire when you decide to stop working. Just because you have money doesn't always equate to a comfortable retirement. Here's why.

A retirement plan achieves two things. First, it brings clarity because you can see exactly what assets you have and how they can work for you. Second, a retirement plan identifies the risks associated with different variables. For example, your health, income, taxes, a divorce, and inflation could factor into a plan.

Your retirement plan brings clarity because you can see all your assets on paper. Next, your financial planner can look at each asset class and determine how they can work for you in retirement. Together, you, your spouse, and your planner can decide how you are going to withdraw from those assets so that you get maximum gain considering inflation, taxation, and other contextual factors. Thus, your retirement plan considers your assets and your retirement outlook under various risk scenarios.

Most people have goals for retirement. Some people want to buy an RV and explore the United States or travel abroad. Others want to sell their home and move closer to their children and grandchildren. Whatever your goals, they come with some amount of cost. We can figure out how to meet those costs when we factor in the risk variables. In short, your retirement plan is the path to realizing your goals in retirement.

One other highly important element of a retirement plan is that it can bring a sense of confidence. I have noticed over the years that most people have retirement goals, but they never attempt to achieve them. Why? Because they don't believe they have enough money to do so. They are fearful that if they do, they won't have enough money to live the life they want or need. A retirement plan gives them the confidence and freedom to pursue their dreams because they know their finances are well-organized and set up for success.

There are many factors to consider when creating a retirement plan. It's not just a matter of how you plan to spend your money, it's also a matter of where your money is coming from currently. We have to manage the source as well as the output.

Some advisors might manage your money for a rate of return only. They may look at your savings and retirement income as a complete fund to manage as a whole without looking at the nuances of where your money is coming from, whether it be from an IRA, rollovers from a 401(k), or brokerage accounts. In my practice, we're different because our planning goes much further and delves into the sources of your funds and looks at how to apply them while incorporating your goals, dreams, wants, and needs. We look at what you want to do and consider the options for paying for them.

At Wealth Shield Financial, we walk our clients through a three-step process.

Our 3 Step Process

Today
DISCOVERY: What you want

We will discuss your current plan and uncover any issues or missed opportunities ...

Together, we will clarify exactly what your goals are.

1 Week
EVALUATION: What you have

We will review what you have and share what we see. Introduction to the Weatlh Shield Action Plan ...

Together, we will determine if we will partner for your retirement.

1 Month
IMPLEMENTATION: What you need

We will design a detailed, easy-to-follow path for pursuing your retirement goals ...

Together, we will implement your Wealth Shield Action Plan.

3 THINGS WE HELP ADDRESS

Income   Taxes   Risk

5 KEY AREAS OF PLANNING

1. **Income**
   - Income and expense analysis
   - Social Security maximization
   - Longevity protection strategies

2. **Investment**
   - Assesing risk tolerance
   - Supported by institutional-level money managers

3. **Tax-Efficient Strategies**
   - Assessing taxable nature of accounts
   - Strategizing ways to include tax-deffered and tax-free money in your plan
   - RMD withdrawal strategy

4. **Health and Long Term Care Strategies**
   - Looking at all aspects of Medicare and supplements
   - Analyzing options for LTC

5. **Estate Planning**
   - Accept and update beneficiaries
   - Have all necessary estate planning documents
   - Legacy maximization

The process begins with crafting your vision for retirement. The rest of the process is designed to find a path to realize that vision. As I mentioned before, in the twenty years I have been advising, I've found that people always have a dream. Let's say they want to retire at sixty-five or seventy and travel around Europe. When I ask what that's going to cost, my clients never have an answer because they haven't planned or budgeted for it. They are living with uncertainty.

I'll go a step further than that and state that failing to plan creates fear. People who don't plan, don't live out their vision because they fear overspending in their early retirement years. People worry that if they overspend in the first ten years of retirement, the last twenty years of their life will be horrible. If you have a plan, you can confidently pursue your dreams knowing that your finances are set. You can visualize the numbers, which we update annually at a minimum, and you will have the confidence to travel the world, move closer to your children and grandchildren, or pursue whatever retirement dreams you have.

A common question is why bother planning for expenses if we don't know whether they'll exist. Won't we be putting aside money for no reason and lose out in the end? My answer is that to feel confident pursuing our dreams in retirement, we need to estimate what your living expenses may be and prepare for the worst-case scenario. Planning for the worst and hoping for the best ensures financial security. It's not difficult to plan realistically and not go too much in the direction of hypotheticals.

Our process takes what we know today about you and your family and we plan around that. We then test the plan using variables that don't match up with today but reveal how your plan would hold up under various scenarios. For example, if inflation is typically 3 percent over a period, we'll use 4 percent to see how your retirement situation changes. If you are currently in a 22 percent tax bracket, we may use a tax bracket of 26 percent or 28 percent to test your financial position and your success in retirement. This type of testing with changing variables builds a robust plan that will stand the test of time and provide the assurance you need to live your life.

The crunching of numbers and myriad scenarios can be overwhelming when you sit down and contemplate them. It's difficult for most people to look at their money objectively and understand what it can and can't do. But for financial professionals, it's not so complex. We have sophisticated software and technology that we use to curate realistic plans from a non-biased position. We generate numerous reports from your data and use them to create a plan for you and you alone.

That's where the planner is of value. We can look at how well you have managed your assets so far and project what your future may look like. We might conclude that you should continue to work for ten more years, but we can no doubt introduce changes today that will make it much more likely that you can retire in ten years. A financial planner can hold your hand and support you through that ten-year timeframe.

We also build a relationship.

That is one factor that distinguishes what we do as financial planners from other planners; the client relationship. Where financial planning is concerned, I think this is a lost art. So many people are turning to robo-advisers or online advisers, but if you ask our clients why they use us, they say, "Matt and his team really care about our family." We get to know our clients on a much more personal level, and I think that that's what really drives the business.

We are good at what we do. We might not be the absolute best at something, but we make up for being second-best in an area because of our personalized approach. We have so much insight into our client's lives and values, we can compensate for any weakness with a strategy that only those close to the family would suggest. For example, we might recommend that the best way to help pay for your grandchild's college is to pay outright versus investing in a college savings plan like a 529. It all depends on the circumstances. We take the time to understand our clients. Most financial firms have access to the same technology and software, so those aren't game changers. The game changer is how you connect with your clients.

Our goal is to alleviate worry. You might feel overwhelmed when you try to piece together all your assets and plan for retirement, but you will feel even more overwhelmed if you don't. Some clients come to see us, and they show us a spreadsheet they've been diligently working on for 20 years, but those clients are rare, Most of our clients tend be W2 workers, who save using a 401(k), IRA, or a Roth IRA and are trying to pay off their mortgage. These clients typically have no idea what their savings equate to or how to plan. With no plan, you have no idea what the future holds. But with a plan, you can relax and not worry if or when the market takes a downturn, inflation is high, or a pandemic like COVID occurs, your plan is a tangible document that shows what you can still do in retirement. Having a plan neutralizes the concern.

The plan that we build with you is a roadmap for success in retirement. It allows you to see what you don't see currently so that you can make adjustments before it's too late. When you reach the age of fifty-five, you have around five to ten years to make adjustments. If you're unsure about something, we can address it and change the roadmap. It puts you in the driver's seat.

When I first started working with these types of plans, my clients were banking executives and the Wall Street community. Wall Street and banking financiers face a particular hurdle in their path to retirement. That is that once they reach age fifty-five, they are considered at the end of the line professionally. By that time, they've had a long career in a bank or on Wall Street, and the tap on the shoulder is imminent because they have become fairly expensive for the bank. They command a high salary, probably a big annual bonus, and have a big title. In the nicest way possible, it's time for them to go. But there's a gap to fill from say age fifty-five to whatever their ultimate retirement age will be. We can advise those finance executives how to manage those years by creating a plan.

We can also change the psyche of the W2 employee to improve the remainder of their working lives. Many W2 workers go to work every day while counting the days until retirement. If we have done the planning process right and they've saved, it shifts the paradigm to one where they can go to work knowing that they can leave tomorrow if they want to. They can go to work with a choice because they know what their numbers are. With no plan, people have no idea when they can retire, and they'll grind it out for another two, three, or five years unnecessarily. In that regard, a plan can be a freeing experience.

Potential Risks to Your Ideal Retirement

Ever feel like life gets in the way and prevents you from doing things you shouldn't ignore? I think if we're honest with ourselves, we've all put off obligations we know are important. In your case, you may be reading this book because it's time to get serious about financial planning and, specifically, devising a way to best prepare for retirement. A retirement plan should be based on more components than just your investments or your finances. The preparation of that strategy begins with your desires, ambitions, and goals for this fulfilling season of life.

There's no such thing as a silly question — not when one of the most common questions we hear from folks regarding retirement is, "Am I going to be okay?" It often seems people are reluctant to meet with financial professionals because they worry they might sound uneducated. However, it's understandable for you to be a novice when it comes to financial issues and retirement concerns. You've been busy with your lives and your careers. Time spent away from work has meant time spent being around those you love and engaging in the activities you enjoy. Retirement provides the opportunity to do even more of that, while not fretting over work obligations.

Concerns people have about what they may encounter during retirement can be far-reaching and still perfectly legitimate. For a quick snapshot, I want to provide a brief sampling of wide-ranging issues that can come up during discussions about what to potentially brace for in retirement. This book will touch on many of these issues in further detail.

Politics: A presidential election often stirs emotions regarding potential effects on the economy. Investors grow anxious about how a new president can influence market returns. It's Congress, however, that establishes tax laws and passes spending bills. Yet the president can indirectly affect the economy and the stock market in various ways such as the appointment of policymakers, development of international relations, and influential sway on new legislation.

Taxes: An example of a president's influence can be cited in signature legislation passed during Donald Trump's presidency, the Tax Cuts and Jobs Act of 2017. However, our tax system remains progressive, so the more you earn, the higher the tax rate within each tax bracket of subsequently higher income. A thorough understanding of tax regulations can be crucial. A financial professional can help identify potential issues a tax professional can help solve.

Inflation: General increases in the prices of goods and services, often measured using the consumer price index (CPI) often stem from fluctuations in real demand for goods and services. Inflation can discourage investment, as well as shortages in goods. A retiree's income can be impacted by the effect inflation can have on a fixed budget. The value of currency decreases because inflation erodes purchasing power.

Cybersecurity: Think you'll give up your smartphone in retirement? No way, right? It's here to stay, along with other intellectual gadgetry, including devices that have not been patented or invented yet. Retirees are becoming more tech-savvy, yet they can also be more trusting, which can be problematic when responding to potential scammers by phone, text, or email. Cybercrime often uses technology to target potential victims. Scammers, much like technology, figure to only grow more sophisticated over time.

CHAPTER 1

Longevity

You would think the prospect of the grave would loom more frightening as we age, yet many retirees say their number one concern is actually running out of money in their twilight years.[1] Unfortunately, this concern is justified because of one significant factor: We're living longer.

According to the Social Security Administration's 2011 Trustee Report, in 1950, the average life expectancy for a sixty-five-year-old man was seventy-eight, and the average for a sixty-five-year-old woman was eighty-one.[2] In the 2023 Trustees Report issued by the SSA, those averages were eighty-six and eighty-three, respectively.[3]

The bottom line of many retirees' budget woes comes down to this: They just didn't plan to live so long. Now, when we are younger and in our working years, that's not something we necessarily see as a bad thing; don't some people fantasize about living forever or, at least, reaching the ripe old age of 100?

---

[1] Brett Arends. MarketWatch. June 5, 2023. "Americans are 'more afraid of running out of money than death'"
https://www.marketwatch.com/story/americans-are-more-afraid-of-running-out-money-than-death-ee5e22e9
[2] ssa.gov. "Actuarial Publications: Cohort Life Expectancy"
https://www.ssa.gov/oact/TR/2011/lr5a4.html
[3] Kay Dee Cole. claritywealthdevelopment.com. July 6, 2022. "What is the Average Life Expectancy for a 65-year-old?"
https://claritywealthdevelopment.com/blog/what-is-the-average-life-expectancy-for-a-65-year-old

However, with a longer lifespan, we face a few snags as we retire. Our resources are finite — we only have so much money to provide income — but our lifespans can be unpredictably long, perhaps longer than our resources allow. Also, longer lives don't necessarily equate with healthier lives. The longer you live, the more money you will likely need to spend on health care, even excluding long-term care needs like nursing homes.

You will also run into inflation. If you don't plan to live another twenty-five years but end up doing so, inflation at an average of 3 percent will approximately double the price of goods over that time period.

Because we don't necessarily get to have our cake and eat it, too, our collective increased longevity hasn't necessarily increased the healthy years of our lives. Typically, our life-extending care most widely applies to the time in our lives when we will need more care in general. Think of common situations like a pacemaker at eighty-five, or cancer treatment at seventy-eight.

"Wow, Matt," I can hear you say. "Way to start with the good news first."

I know, I've painted a grim picture, but all I'm concerned about here is cost. It's hard to put a dollar sign on life, but that is essentially what we're talking about when discussing longevity and finances. Living longer isn't a bad thing; it just costs more, and one key to a sound retirement strategy is preparing for it in advance.

Ken came to us around twelve years ago. He worked for a large shipping company. He and his wife were good savers, but Ken wasn't sure when he could retire, so he continued to work. After a few years, his company was acquired, and Ken was let go. The market timing was favorable when we first saw him as a client because we were in the midst of a bull market for the last ten years. Ken was in an extremely good position because his savings were mostly market-based assets.

Then, Ken inherited a substantial sum when his wife's mother passed away. The couple had barely any expenses, so Ken and his wife found themselves spending far less than they were earning in interest and continuing to add to the bottom line of their retirement plan. Unfortunately, Ken's wife passed away from cancer. Because our planning included life insurance, Ken inherited even more money tax-free after the passing of his wife

Some ten years into our client relationship with Ken, he now has a new partner and has an incredible amount of money. He's enjoying a wonderful retirement doing all the things he wanted to. Even with our retirement planning, we never thought Ken would be as financially healthy as he is.

We also looked at Ken's legacy. We did some planning for his three children and his future grandchildren. We set up a trust for each child and funded the trusts with the money Ken had gained from his wife's life insurance. With his legacy taken care of, Ken is enjoying his retirement without worrying about overspending. His wealth is continuing to grow while he's chasing his dreams, and he has secured a legacy for his children and grandchildren.

Part of the planning process is re-orienting when life events occur. When Ken's wife passed, it was a shock. Ken needed some time to reevaluate. He no longer had joint goals with his wife, and he had to decide what to do with the money he gained. Would he stay in the same house, for example? The planning process we had followed had already considered the longevity of Ken and his wife, and those provisions ensured Ken could get on with his life and make the right decisions.

Living longer may be more expensive, but it can be so meaningful when you plan for your "just-in-cases."

Retiring Early

A key part of planning for retirement revolves around retirement income. After all, retirement is cutting the cord that tethers you to your employer — and your monthly check. However, that check often comes with many other benefits, particularly health care. Health care is often the thing that can unexpectedly put dreams for an early retirement on hold. Some employers offer health benefits to their retired workers, but that number has declined drastically over the past several decades.

In 1988, among employers who offered health benefits to their workers, 66 percent offered health benefits to their retirees. That number has since dwindled to 21 percent[4] So, with employer-offered retirement health benefits on the wane, this becomes a major point of concern for anyone who is looking to retire, particularly those who are looking to retire before age sixty-five, when they would become eligible for Medicare coverage.

Fidelity estimates that the average retired couple at age sixty-five will need approximately $315,000 for health care expenses in retirement, not including long-term care.[5] Do you think it's likely that cost will decrease?

Even if you are working until age sixty-five or have plans to cover your health expenses until that point, I often have clients who incorrectly assume Medicare is their golden ticket to cover all expenses. That is simply not the case.

Retiring Later

Planning for a long life in retirement partly depends on when you retire. While many people end up retiring earlier than they anticipated — due to injuries, layoffs, family crises, and other unforeseen circumstances — continuing to work past age sixty (and even sixty-five) is still a viable option for others and can be an excellent way to help establish financial confidence in retirement.

---

[4] Henry J. Kaiser Family Foundation. October 27, 2022. "2022 Employer Health Benefits Survey Section Eleven: Retiree Health Benefits" https://www.kff.org/report-section/ehbs-2022-section-11-retiree-health-benefits/

[5] Fidelity Viewpoints. Fidelity. August 29, 2022. "How to Plan for Rising Health Care Costs" https://www.fidelity.com/viewpoints/personal-finance/plan-for-rising-health-care-costs

There are many reasons for this. For one, you obviously still earn a paycheck and the benefits accompanying it. Medical coverage and beefing up your retirement accounts with further savings can be significant by themselves, but continuing to generate income should also keep you from dipping into your retirement funds, further allowing them the opportunity to grow.

Additionally, for many workers, their nine-to-five job is more than just clocking in and out. Having a sense of purpose can keep us active physically, mentally, and socially. That kind of activity and level of engagement may also help stave off many of the health problems that plague retirees. Avoiding a sedentary life is one of the advantages of staying plugged into the workforce, if possible.

Joe is an example of someone who needed to stay "plugged in." Joe became a client around three years ago. He was a retired orthopedic doctor and was winding down his practice in New Jersey. Joe made our job easy by laying everything out on the table regarding his assets. We quickly realized that Joe had significant net worth; however, much of it was tied up in real estate. There was little liquid capital because Joe was no longer practicing.

We advised that he needed to sell some of his properties to create some liquidity so that he could pay his mortgages and continue to support his adult children. We also advised selling his New Jersey residence. Joe was spending little time in New Jersey where the cost of owning a property is high, so he sold his home in the height of the market, and we repurposed a portion of that money by investing in annuities to provide income using the balance to reduce his debt.

Joe had reduced his fixed costs and was no longer paying high New Jersey taxes. He moved to South Carolina where the cost of living is much lower. Retirement was no longer difficult for Joe, however, because he was bored. He didn't want to be a business owner again, so he found a role assisting a younger orthopedic doctor three days a week. He's content now, and still "plugged in."

Health Care

Take a second to reflect on your health care plan. Although working up to or even past age sixty-five could allow you to avoid a coverage gap between your working years and Medicare, that may not be an option for you. Even if it is, when you retire, you will need to make some decisions about what kind of insurance coverage you may need to supplement your Medicare. Are there any medical needs you have that may require coverage in addition to Medicare? Did your parents or grandparents have any inherited medical conditions you might consider using a special savings plan to cover?

These are all questions that are important to review with your financial professional so you can be sure you have enough money put aside for health care.

Long-Term Care

Longevity means the need for long-term care is statistically more likely to happen. If you intend to pass on a legacy, planning for long-term care is paramount, since most estimates project nearly 70 percent of Americans who reach age sixty-five will need some type of it.[6] However, this may be one of the biggest, most stressful pieces of longevity planning I encounter in my work. For one thing, who wants to talk about the point in their lives when they may feel the most limited? Who wants to dwell on what will happen if they can no longer toilet, bathe, dress, or feed themselves?

I get it; this is a less-than-fun part of planning. But a little bit of preparation now can go a long way!

When it comes to your longevity, just like with your goals, one of the important things to do is sit and dream. It may not

---

[6] Claire Samuels. aPlaceforMom.com. September 13, 2023. "Long-Term Care Statistics: A Portrait of Americans in Assisted Living, Nursing Homes, and Skilled Nursing Facilities" https://www.aplaceformom.com/senior-living-data/articles/long-term-care-statistics

be the fun, road-trip-to-the-Grand-Canyon kind of dreaming, but you can spend time envisioning how you want your twilight years to look.

For instance, if it is important for you to live in your home for as long as possible, who will provide for the day-to-day fixes and to-dos of housework if you become ill? Will you set aside money for a service, or do you have relatives or friends nearby whom you could comfortably allow to help you? Do you prefer in-home care over a nursing home or assisted living? This could be a good time to discuss the possibility of moving into a retirement community versus staying where you are or whether it's worth moving to another state and leaving relatives behind.

These are all important factors to discuss with your spouse and children, as *now* is the right time to address questions and concerns. For instance, is aging in place more important to one spouse than the other? Are the friends or relatives who live nearby emotionally, physically, and financially capable of helping you for a time if you face an illness?

Many families I meet with find these conversations very uncomfortable, particularly when children discuss nursing home care with their parents. A knee-jerk reaction for many is to promise they will care for their aging parents. This is noble and well-intentioned, but there needs to be an element of realism here. Does "help" from an adult child mean they stop by and help you with laundry, cooking, home maintenance, and bills? Or does it mean they move you into their spare room when you have hip surgery? Are they prepared to help you use the restroom and bathe if that becomes difficult for you to do on your own?

I don't mean to discourage families from caring for their own; this can be a profoundly admirable relationship when it works out. However, I've seen families put off planning for late-in-life care based on a tenuous promise that the adult children would care for their parents, only to watch as the support system crumbles. Sometimes, this is because the assumed caregiver hasn't given serious thought to the preparation they would need, both in a formal sense and regarding their personal physical, emotional, and financial commitments. This is often also because we can't see the future: Alzheimer's disease and other maladies of old age can exact a heavy toll. When a loved one reaches the point where they are at risk of wandering away or need help with two or more activities of daily living, it can be more than one person or a family can realistically handle.

If you know what you want, communicate with your family about both the best-case and worst-case scenarios. Then, hope for the best, and plan for the worst.

Realistic Cost of Care

Included in your planning should be a consideration for the cost of long-term care. The potential costs for such care and treatment can be underestimated, especially by those who have maintained robust health and find it difficult to envision future declines in their condition.

Another piece of planning for long-term care costs is anticipating inflation. It's common knowledge that prices have been and keep rising, which can lower your purchasing power on everything from food to medical care. Long-term care is a big piece of the inflation-disparity pie.

While local costs vary from state to state, the following table shows the national median for various forms of long-term care (plus projections that account for a 3 percent annual inflation, so you can see what I am referencing):[7]

---

[7] Nationwide. 2022. "Compare Long-term Care costs from state to state" https://nationwidefinancialltcmap.hvsfinancial.com/

Long-Term Care Costs: Inflation				
	Informal Care	Home Care	Assisted Living	Nursing Home (semi-private room)
Annual 2024	$42,037	$33,621	$60,874	$113,522
Annual 2034	$56,495	$45,184	$81,810	$160,134
Annual 2044	$75,924	$60,723	$109,945	$225,884
Annual 2054	$102,036	$81,607	$147,757	$318,632

[8]

Fund Your Long-Term Care

One common mistake I see occurs in those who haven't planned for long-term care because they assume the government will provide everything. But that's a big misconception. The government has two health insurance programs: Medicare and Medicaid. These can greatly assist you in your health care *needs* in retirement but usually don't provide enough coverage to cover all your health care *costs* in retirement. My firm isn't a government outpost, so we don't get to make decisions regarding policy and specifics about either of these programs. I'm going to give an overview of both, but if you want to dive into the details of these programs, you can visit www.Medicare.gov and www.Medicaid.gov.

---

[8] Ibid.

Medicare

Medicare covers those aged sixty-five and older and those who are disabled. Medicare's coverage of any nursing-home-related health issues is limited. It might cover your nursing home stay if it is not a "custodial" stay and isn't long-term. For example, if you break a bone or suffer a stroke, stay in a nursing home for rehabilitative care, and then return home, Medicare may cover you. However, if you have developed dementia or are looking to move to a nursing facility because you can no longer bathe, dress, toilet, feed yourself, or take care of your hygiene, etc., then Medicare is not going to pay for your nursing home costs.[9]

You can enroll in Medicare anytime during the three months before and three months after your sixty-fifth birthday. Miss your enrollment deadline, and you could risk paying increased premiums for the rest of your life.[10] On top of prompt enrollment, there are a few other things to think about when it comes to Medicare, not least among them being the need to understand the different "parts," what they do, and what they don't cover.

Part A

Medicare Part A is what you might think of as "classic" Medicare. Hospital care, some types of home health care, and major medical care fall under this. While most enrollees pay nothing for this service (as they likely paid into the system for at least ten years), you might have to, based on either work history or delayed signup. In 2024, the highest premium is $505 per month, and a hospital stay does have a deductible —

---

[9] Medicare.gov. "What Part A covers" https://www.medicare.gov/what-medicare-covers/part-a/what-part-a-covers.html
[10] Medicare.gov. "When can I sign up for Medicare?" https://www.medicare.gov/basics/get-started-with-medicare/sign-up/when-can-i-sign-up-for-medicare

$1,632.[11] Also, if you have a hospital stay that surpasses sixty days, you could be looking at additional costs; keep in mind, Medicare doesn't pay for long-term care and services.

Part B

Medicare Part B is an essential piece of wrap-around coverage for Medicare Part A. It helps pay for doctor visits and outpatient services. This also comes with a price tag: Although the Part B annual deductible is only $240 in 2024, you will still pay 20 percent of all costs after that, with no limit on out-of-pocket expenses. The Part B monthly premium for 2024 ranges from the standard amount of $174.70 to $594.[12]

Part C

Medicare Part C (more commonly known as a Medicare Advantage plan) is an alternative to a combination of Parts A, B, and sometimes D. Administered through private insurance companies, these have a variety of costs and restrictions, and they are subject to the specific policies and rules of the issuing carrier.

Part D

Medicare Part D is also offered through a private insurer and is supplemental to Parts A and B, as its primary purpose is to cover prescription drugs. Like any private insurance plan, Part D has its quirks and rules that vary from insurer to insurer.

---

[11] CMS.gov. October 12, 2023. "2024 Medicare Parts A & B Premiums and Deductibles" https://www.cms.gov/newsroom/fact-sheets/2024-medicare-parts-b-premiums-and-deductibles?ref=biztoc.com
[12] Ibid.

The Donut Hole

Even with a "Part D" in place, you may still have a coverage gap between what your Part D private drug insurance pays for your prescription and what basic Medicare pays. In 2024, the coverage gap is $5,030, meaning that after you meet your private prescription insurance limit, you will spend no more than 25 percent of your drug costs out-of-pocket before Medicare kicks in to pay for more prescription drugs.[13]

Note: In the donut hole, you pay up to 25 percent out of pocket for all covered medications. You leave the donut hole once you've spent $8,000 out of pocket for covered drugs in 2024. 2024 is the last year for the donut hole. A $2,000 out-of-pocket cap takes effect for Medicare Part D in 2025.

Medicare Supplements

Medicare Supplement Insurance, MedSupp, Medigap, or plans labeled Medicare Part F, G, H, I, J ... Known by a variety of monikers, this is just a fancy way of saying "medical coverage for those over sixty-five that picks up the tab for whatever the federal Medicare program(s) doesn't." Again, costs, limitations, etc., vary by carrier.

Does that sound like a bunch of government alphabet soup to you? It certainly does to me. And did you read the fine print? Unpredictable costs, varied restrictions, difficult-to-compare benefits, donut holes, and coverage gaps. That's par for the course with health care plans throughout our adult lives. What gives? I thought Medicare was supposed to be easier, comprehensive, and at no cost!

The truth is there is probably no stage of life when health care is easy to understand. My mother passed away when she was sixty-six years old from cancer. When she was sixty-five and trying to understand Medicare, I knew that it wasn't my

---

[13] Medicare. "Costs in the coverage gap" https://www.medicare.gov/drug-coverage-part-d/costs-for-medicare-drug-coverage/costs-in-the-coverage-gap

specialty, so we found an expert to help her. Medicare and Medicaid are two universes all of their own. I recommend finding an expert in that field to help you decide which coverage to choose. We partner with another firm for Medicare planning because it's too far beyond the macro planning that we do. It's a difficult space to navigate, particularly if you have health changes. I learned from the experience with my mother that finding a professional and partnering with that professional is the best path forward.

One of the best things you can do for yourself is to scope out the health care field early, compare costs often, and prepare for out-of-pocket costs well in advance — decades, if possible.

Medicaid

Medicaid is a program the states administer, so funding, protocol, and limitations vary. Compared to Medicare, Medicaid more widely covers nursing home care, but it targets a different demographic: those with low incomes.

If you have more assets than the Medicaid limit in your state and need nursing home care, you will need to use those assets to pay for your care. You will also have a list of additional state-approved ways to use or spend some of these assets over the Medicaid limit, such as pre-purchasing burial plots and funeral expenses or paying off debts. After that, your remaining assets fund your nursing home stay until they are gone, at which point Medicaid will jump in.

Some people aren't stymied by this, thinking they will just pass on their financial assets early by gifting them to relatives, friends, and causes so they can qualify for Medicaid when they need it. However, to prevent this exact scenario, Uncle Sam has implemented what's called the "look-back period." Currently, if you enroll in Medicaid, you are subject to having the government scrutinize the last five years of your finances for large gifts or expenses that may subject you to penalties, temporarily making you ineligible for Medicaid coverage.

So, if you're planning to preserve your money for future generations and retain control of your financial resources during your lifetime, you'll probably want to prepare for the costs of longevity beyond a "government plan."

Self-Funding

One way to fund a longer life is the old-fashioned way, through self-funding. There are a variety of financial tools you can use, and they all have their pros and cons. If your assets are in low-interest financial vehicles (savings, bonds, CDs), you risk letting inflation erode the value of your dollar. If you are relying on the stock market, you have more growth potential, but you'll also want to consider the possible implications of market volatility. What if your assets take a hit? If you suffer a loss in your retirement portfolio in early or mid-retirement, you might have the option to "tighten your belt," so to speak, and cut back on discretionary spending to allow your portfolio the room to bounce back. But if you are retired and depend on income from a stock account that just hit a downward stride, what are you going to do?

HSAs

These days, you might also be able to self-fund through a health savings account (HSA) if you have access to one through a high-deductible health plan (you will not qualify to save in an HSA after enrolling in Medicare). In an HSA, any growth of your tax-deductible contributions will be tax-free, and any distributions paid out for qualified health costs are also tax-free. Long-term care expenses count as health costs, so if this is an option available to you, it is one way to use the tax advantages to self-fund your longevity. Bear in mind if you are younger than sixty-five, any money you use for non-qualified expenses will be subject to taxes and penalties, and if you are older than sixty-five, any HSA money you use for non-medical expenses is subject to income tax.

LTCI

One slightly more nuanced way to pay for longevity — specifically for long-term care — is long-term care insurance (LTCI). As car insurance protects your assets in case of a car accident and home insurance protects your assets in case something happens to your house, long-term care insurance aims to protect your assets in case you need long-term care in an at-home or nursing home situation.

As with other types of insurance, you will pay a monthly or annual premium in exchange for an insurance company paying for long-term care down the road. Typically, policies cover two to three years of care, which is adequate for an "average" situation: it's estimated that 70 percent of Americans aged sixty-five and older will need long-term care of some kind.[14]

Now, there are a few oft-cited components of LTCI that make it unattractive for some:

- Expense — LTCI can be expensive. It is generally less expensive the younger you are, but a sixty-five-year-old couple who purchased LTCI in 2023 could expect to pay a combined annual amount of $3,750 for a policy. And the annual cost only increases from there the older you are.[15]
- Limited options — LTCI may be expensive for consumers, but it can also be expensive for companies that offer it. With fewer companies willing to take on that expense, the market narrows, meaning opportunities to price shop for policies with different options or custom benefits are limited.

---

[14] Claire Samuels. aplaceformom.com. September 13, 2023. "Portrait of Americans in Assisted Living, Nursing Homes, and Skilled Nursing Facilities" https://www.aplaceformom.com/senior-living-data/articles/long-term-care-statistics

[15] American Association for Long-Term Care Insurance. 2023. "Long-Term Care Insurance Facts – Data – Statistics – 2023 Reports" https://www.aaltci.org/long-term-care-insurance/learning-center/ltcfacts-2023.php

- If you know you need it, you might not be able to get it — Insurance companies offering LTCI are taking on a risk that you may need LTCI. That risk is the foundation of the product — you may or may not need it. If you know you will need it because you have a dementia diagnosis or another illness for which you will need long-term care, you will likely not qualify for LTCI coverage.
- Use it or lose it — If you have LTCI and are in the minority of Americans who die having never needed long-term care, all the money you paid into your LTCI policy is gone.
- Possibly fluctuating rates — Your premium rate is not locked in on LTCI. Companies maintain the ability to raise or lower your premium amounts. This means some seniors face an ultimatum: Keep funding a policy at what might be a less affordable rate *or* lose coverage and let go of all the money they have paid so far.

After that, you might be thinking, "How can people possibly be interested in LTCI?" But let me repeat myself — it's anticipated that as many as 70 percent of Americans will need long-term care. And although only one in ten Americans aged fifty-five-plus has purchased LTCI, keep in mind the high cost of nursing home care. Can you afford $7,000 a month to put into nursing home care and still have enough left over to protect your legacy? This is a very real concern, considering one set of statistics reported a two-in-three chance that a senior citizen will become physically or cognitively impaired in their lifetime.[16] So, not to sound like a broken record, but it is vitally important to have a plan in place to deal with longevity and long-term care, especially if you intend to leave a financial legacy.

We offer long-term care insurance at Wealth Shield Financial because I would not be a holistic planner if I didn't. But we also

---

[16] payingforseniorcare.com. 2022. "Long-Term Senior Care Statistics" https://www.payingforseniorcare.com/statistics

show how to mitigate the cost. We show you what's available in the market and then decide if it makes sense based on whether you have enough assets to self-insure. Many people don't have enough money to self-insure, but they don't have funds sidelined and earmarked for that rainy day when a long-term care event strikes them or their spouse. It costs a lot of money when that happens, and if you can use somebody else's money, that makes more sense.

A few relevant statistics to keep in mind:
- The longer you live, the more health care you will likely need to pay for.
- The average cost of a private nursing home room in the United States between 2022 and 2023 was $9,034 a month.[17] But keep in mind, that is just the nursing home — it doesn't include other medical costs, let alone pleasantries like entertainment or hobby spending.
- As referenced earlier, Fidelity calculated in a 2022 study that a healthy couple retiring at age sixty-five could expect to pay around $315,000 over the course of retirement to cover health and medical expenses.

I know. "Whoa, there, Matt, I was hoping to have a realistic idea of health costs, not be driven over by a cement mixer!"

The good news is, while we don't know these exact costs in advance, we know there *will* be costs. And you won't have to pay your total Medicare lifetime premiums in one day as a lump sum. Now that you have a good idea of health care costs in retirement, you can *plan* for them! That's the real point here: Planning in advance can keep you from feeling nickel-and-dimed to your wits' end. Instead, having a sizeable portion of your assets earmarked for health care can allow you the

---

[17] Chacour Koop. aPlaceforMom.com. September 15, 2023. "Average Cost of Long-Term Care: A State-by-State Guide to Senior Care in the U.S." https://www.aplaceformom.com/senior-living-data/articles/average-cost-long-term-care

freedom to choose health care networks, coverage options, and long-term care possibilities that you like.

Product Riders

LTCI and self-funding are not the only ways to plan for the expenses of longevity. Some companies are getting creative with their products, particularly insurance companies. One way they are retooling to meet people's needs is through optional product riders on annuities and life insurance. Elsewhere in this book, I talk about annuity basics, but here's a brief overview: Annuities are insurance contracts. You pay the insurance company a premium — either as a lump sum or as a series of payments over a set amount of time — in exchange for guaranteed income payments.

One of the advantages of an annuity is it has access to riders, which allow you to tweak your contract for a fee — typically ranging from 0.1 percent to 1 percent of the contract value annually[18]. One annuity rider some companies offer is a long-term care rider. If you have an annuity with a long-term care rider and are not in need of long-term care, your contract behaves as any annuity contract would — nothing changes.

Generally speaking, if you reach a point when you can't perform multiple functions of daily life on your own, you notify the insurance company, and a representative will turn on those provisions of your contract, and if you meet the long-term care rider requirements, your additional rider benefits can be activated to help you pay for your long-term care needs. An insurance company representative will turn on those provisions of your contract. Activating LTC rider benefits is more involved than simply calling your insurance carrier. A physician must confirm that you cannot perform the required amount of activities of daily living (ADLs).

---

[18] Shawn Plummer. The Annuity Expert. 2024. "Annuity Fees: What You Need To Know" https://www.annuityexpertadvice.com/types-of-annuities/annuity-fees/

Like LTCI, different companies and products offer different options. Some annuity long-term care riders offer coverage of two years in a nursing home situation. Others cap expenses at two times the original annuity's value. It greatly depends. Some people prefer this option because there isn't a "use-it-or-lose-it" piece; if you die without ever having needed long-term care, you still will have had the income benefit from the base contract.

Still, as with any annuities or insurance contracts, there are the usual restrictions and limitations. Withdrawing money from the contract will affect future income payments, early distributions can result in a penalty, income taxes may apply, and, because the insurance company's solvency is what guarantees your payments, it's important to do your research about the insurance company you are considering purchasing a contract from.

Understandably, a discussion on long-term care is bound to feel at least a little tedious. Yet, this is an important piece of planning for income in retirement, particularly if you want to leave a legacy.

If you sat forty pre-retirees in a room, they could probably all tell you of an event where a relative ended up needing round-the-clock care for years, and it cost a fortune. Our firm doesn't have direct experience of that because we head off the problem as early as possible. Long-term care, when it really goes wrong, can wipe out a retirement plan. It's the one variable that people don't think about, but it's also the biggest outlier. It could amount to $500,000 or a million dollars. Most people can't live out a reasonable retirement while paying that type of money.

Spousal Planning

Here's one thing to keep in mind no matter how you plan to save: Many of us will be planning for more than ourselves. Look back at all the stats on health events and the likelihood of long life and long-term care. If they hold true for a single individual, then the likelihood of having a costly health or long-term care event is even higher for a married couple. You'll be planning for not just one life, but two. So, when it comes to long-term care insurance, annuities, self-funding, or whatever strategy you are looking at using, be sure you are funding longevity for the both of you.

CHAPTER 2

Taxes

Where to begin with taxes? Perhaps by acknowledging we all bear responsibility for the resources we share such as. roads, bridges, and schools. Every American's patriotic duty is to pay their fair share of taxes. Many would agree with me. However, while they don't mind paying their fair share, they're not interested in paying one cent more than that!

Now, just talking about taxes probably takes your mind to April — tax season. You are probably thinking about all the forms you collect and how you file. Perhaps you are thinking about your certified public accountant or another qualified tax professional and saying to yourself, "I've already got taxes taken care of, thanks!"

However, what I see when people come into my office is that their relationship with their tax professional is purely a January through April relationship. That means they may have a tax *professional,* but not a tax *planner*.

What I mean is tax planning extends beyond filing taxes. In April, we are required to settle our accounts with the IRS to make sure we have paid up on our bill or even the score if we have overpaid. But real tax planning is about making each financial move in a way that allows you to keep the most money in your pocket and out of Uncle Sam's.

Now, as a caveat, I want to emphasize I am neither a CPA nor a tax planner, but I see the way taxes affect my clients, and I have plenty of experience helping clients implement tax-efficient strategies in their retirement plans in conjunction with their tax professionals.

We've had a strategic partnership for fifteen years with a third-party CPA firm. The company is run by three brothers, who are CPAs. The business was started by their parents, who were also CPAs, so it's a family business, like us, that reflects our values. If our clients want specific help on taxes beyond the advice we can give them in our office, we refer them to the CPAs, or we might schedule a conference call or a Zoom meeting to delve deeper into tax planning. It is especially important to me to help my clients develop tax-efficient strategies in their retirement plans because each dollar they can keep in their pockets is a dollar we can put to work.

We see a lot of success with the third-party CPA firm with our self-employed clients or business owners. That's because there is more opportunity inside the tax code for business owners than for W2 workers. For W2 employees, taxes play a huge role in retirement because if you don't do any tax planning, the government will take whatever they can. That could be 20 percent, 30 percent, or it could be as high as 40 percent of your revenues. You can't beat 40 percent with a rate of return. If the government's taking 40 percent, and the market's giving you 10 percent, you're losing significant money. While more can be done for the self-employed, W2 workers can mitigate their losses by doing some tax planning. In some cases, W2 workers can save hundreds of thousands of dollars in taxes.

For small business owners, we have installed quite a few retirement plans that significantly reduce their current tax liability. We focus on how to reduce their future tax liabilities because whatever you can save today usually sets you up for a tax bill tomorrow. We look for a balance between how much a client should save today vs. how much they will have to pay later in life. This is a critical issue because we don't know what the tax rates will be in the future.

The Fed

Now, in the United States, taxes can be a rather uncertain proposition. Depending on who is in the White House and which party controls Congress, we might be tempted to assume tax rates could either decline or increase in the next four to eight years accordingly. However, there is one (large!) factor we, as a nation, must confront: the national debt.

Currently, according to USDebtClock.org, we are over $34,000,000,000,000 in debt and climbing. That's $34 *trillion* with a "T." With just $1 trillion, you could park it in the bank at a zero percent interest rate and spend more than $54 million every day for fifty years without hitting a zero balance.

Even if Congress got a handle and stopped that debt from its daily compound, divided by each taxpayer, we each would owe about $267,000. So, will that be check, cash, or Venmo?[19]

My point here isn't to give you anxiety. I'm just cautioning you that even with the rosiest of outlooks on our personal income tax rates, none of us should count on low tax rates for the long term. Instead, you and your network of professionals (tax, legal, and financial) should constantly be looking for ways to take advantage of tax-saving opportunities as they come.

So, how can we get started?

Know Your Limits

One of the foundational pieces of tax planning is knowing and understanding your marginal tax rate. Marginal tax rate is the tax rate you pay on your highest dollar of income. In the United States, we use a progressive tax system, meaning your marginal tax rate increases as your taxable income increases. However, to be clear, not all of your income is taxed at that highest rate — only the upper portion.

---

[19] usdebtclock.org. Accessed on March 27, 2024.

A taxpayer's income is divided into tax brackets, and the brackets determine the rate applied to increments of the filer's taxable income.

For example, if your single friend tells you she is in the 22 percent tax bracket, that means her highest amount of income is taxed at 22 percent, but chunks of her income are taxed at lower rates. Using the 2024 tax bracket below, her first $11,600 of income will be taxed at 10 percent, but her next chunk of income ($11,601 to $47,150) will be taxed at 12 percent. Finally, her income, beginning at $47,151, will be taxed at 22 percent. Her tax owed for the year — before any additional taxes or credits — is the accumulation of those three amounts.

2024 Tax Brackets: Single Filers		
Tax Rate	Taxable Income Bracket	Tax Owed
10%	$0 to $11,600	10% of taxable income.
12%	$11,601 to $47,150	$1,160 plus 12% of the amount over $11,600
22%	$47,151 to $100,525	$5,426 plus 22% of the amount over $47,150
24%	$100,526 to $191,950	$17,168.50 plus 24% of the amount over $100,525
32%	$191,951 to $243,725	$39,110.50 plus 32% of the amount over $191,950
35%	$243,726 to $609,350	$55,678.50 plus 35% of the amount over $243,725
37%	$609,351 or more	$183,647.25 plus 37% of the amount over $609,350

[20]

It's important to note the difference between marginal and effective tax rates. The effective tax rate represents the percentage of taxable income an individual pays in taxes. To calculate the effective rate, take the total dollar amount you pay in income tax and divide it by your total income. Thus, it is the average rate and is almost always a lower percentage than a marginal rate.

Why are marginal and effective rates important in retirement planning? Federal income tax is often one of the

---

[20] Sabrina Parys and Tina Orem. Nerdwallet. November 14, 2023. "2023-2024 Tax Brackets and Federal Income Tax Rates" https://www.nerdwallet.com/article/taxes/federal-income-tax-brackets

biggest expenses individuals pay in their lives. Granted, there are federal tax breaks for Americans over the age of sixty-five. In 2024, those deductions amounted to $1,550 for married people filing jointly or separately, and $1,950 for a single person or head of household.[21]

However, many former high-income earners continue to pay income taxes. Estimating your marginal tax rate is one of the components in determining when to begin Social Security and a crucial factor regarding Roth IRA conversions. Also, a thorough analysis of current and future marginal tax rates is important in the strategic planning for required minimum distributions (RMDs) on tax-deferred retirement accounts.

Assuming a Lower Tax Rate

Retirement has always been imagined as a time when you stop working and no longer earn wages or self-employment income. In the past, Social Security benefits were not subject to taxation. Even though pensions were usually taxable, their income stream didn't fully replace a recipient's previous salary. If you needed to pull from your investment funds during retirement, keep in mind that the principal had already been taxed. In general, prior to the 1970s, your income during retirement — your cash inflow — was usually taxed at a lower rate than when you were working because you had less income and certain portions of it were not taxable.

In 1978, lawmakers created Section 401 of the Internal Revenue Code to prevent companies from using tax-advantaged profit-sharing plans to primarily benefit executives. However, businessman Ted Benna reimagined this code as the foundation of the modern 401(k). This innovation ultimately led to the decline of traditional company pension plans, while shifting both control and risk to employees. The most significant change was the shift of taxation from when

---

[21] Janet Berry-Johnson. Forbes.com. December 4, 2023. "Standard Deductions for 2023 and 2024 Tax Returns, and Extra Benefits for People Over 65" https://www.forbes.com/advisor/taxes/standard-deduction/

employees were paid and when investment income was earned to the time of withdrawal. This tax advantage encouraged individuals to save more money in tax-deferred plans than they would have in regular savings accounts, up to the allowed limits.

In addition, in 1983, Social Security introduced new tax brackets to address the problem of decreasing reserves. This resulted in both the potential for Social Security to become taxable and a significant shift in retirement planning strategy. Within a five-year period, the retirement planning landscape changed for decades going forward, possibly forever.

A big selling point for qualified retirement accounts (401(k)s, 403(b)s, IRAs, etc.) is the theory that people will pay less in tax during their retirement years than during their working years when they're putting that money away. The idea is that you're allowed to "defer" paying the tax on that income until your marginal tax rate drops in retirement. Hence, you pay less in tax on that income.

But what if it doesn't pan out that way? For some retirees, their marginal tax rate will stay the same in retirement or even increase. If you have a healthy balance in your qualified retirement account, combining its RMDs or even a Roth conversion with Social Security can result in what is called the "tax torpedo." This tax increase occurs when a larger percent of your Social Security becomes taxable, and that same income increase consequently bumps a taxpayer up to a higher marginal rate.

401(k)/IRA/Roth IRA

One sometimes-unexpected piece of tax planning in retirement concerns the 401(k) or IRA. Most of us have one of these accounts or an equivalent. We pay in throughout our working lives, dutifully socking away a portion of our earnings in these tax-deferred accounts. There's the rub: tax-*deferred*, not tax-*free*. Very rarely is anything free of taxation when you get down to it. Using 401(k)s and IRAs in retirement is no different. The taxes the government deferred when you were in your working years are now coming due, and you will pay taxes on that income at whatever your current tax rate is.

Just to ensure Uncle Sam gets his due, the government also has an RMD rule. Beginning at age seventy-three (or seventy-five if you were born in 1960 or after), you are required to withdraw a certain minimum amount every year from your 401(k) or IRA, or else you will face a tax penalty on any RMD monies you should have withdrawn but didn't — and that's on top of income tax. The SECURE Act 2.0 reduced the penalty to 25 percent (from 50 percent). Timely corrections also can further reduce the penalty to 10 percent.[22]

Of course, there is also the Roth account. You can think of the difference between a Roth and a traditional retirement account as the difference between taxing the seed and taxing the harvest. Because Roths get funded with post-tax dollars, there aren't tax penalties for early withdrawals of the principal, nor are there taxes on the growth after you reach age fifty-nine-and-one-half. Perhaps best of all, there are no RMDs. Of course, you must own a Roth account for a minimum of five years before you are able to take advantage of all its features.

This is one more area where it pays to be aware of your marginal tax rate. Some people may opt to put any excess RMDs from their traditional retirement accounts into stocks or insurance. Others may find it advantageous to "convert" their traditional retirement account funds to Roth account funds in a year during which they are in a lower tax bracket.

Roth IRA Conversions

A Roth conversion simply means converting (or withdrawing) monies from your traditional, tax-deferred retirement accounts and moving them to a Roth account. Once inside the Roth, any

---

[22] Jim Probasco. Investopedia.com. January 6, 2023. "SECURE 2.0 Act of 2022." https://www.investopedia.com/secure-2-0-definition-5225115

growth on these funds will accumulate completely tax-free, and tax will not be owed when the Roth funds are withdrawn assuming the conditions noted above. This is an exciting opportunity for accumulation! However, a thoughtful strategy is beneficial in the conversion process. Since dollars were placed into the traditional account pre-tax and the growth is taxable in these accounts, tax is owed on *all* the money converted to the Roth. Converting an employer plan account to a Roth IRA is a taxable event. Increased taxable income from the Roth IRA conversion may have several consequences, including (but not limited to) a need for additional tax withholding or estimated tax payments, the loss of certain tax deductions and credits, higher taxes on Social Security benefits, and higher Medicare premiums.

Points to consider regarding a conversion:

How are you going to pay the tax? Again, any time you withdraw funds from a 401(k) or traditional IRA, tax is owed on 100 percent of that money, whether the distribution was a basic withdrawal, an RMD, or a Roth conversion. In addition to the income tax, if the account owner is younger than fifty-nine-and-one-half, it is most likely a 10 percent tax penalty will be accessed. So, if you're under fifty-nine-and-one-half and have a year when your income is lower – reducing your marginal tax rate – you need to weigh the amount of the tax penalty against the decrease in ordinary income tax.

As a tricky sidenote, if you are under fifty-nine-and-one-half and you have tax withheld from your conversion and sent directly to the government, you will not escape the 10 percent penalty.

Did you compare your current tax rate to your estimated future rate? As mentioned above, a good time to consider a Roth is in a year when your taxable income — and thus your marginal tax rate — is lower than normal or lower than expected in the future. A popular conversion strategy is to transfer funds during a period referred to as "the trough years." That is the period after you've retired but before you begin receiving Social Security or are required to begin RMDs. It is easier to manage the tax on the conversion during these years as you have more control over the sources and the amounts of your income.

What is your Roth withdrawal strategy? There are four considerations here.

- Can you leave converted money in the Roth for at least five years? You must leave your converted money in the Roth for at least five years for the withdrawals to be tax-free. That five-year countdown begins on January 1 of the year you made the conversion, even if your conversion date was December 31. This five-year countdown applies in each year you make a conversion.
- Even if you hold the Roth funds for five years, you will still face penalties for withdrawals if you're under fifty-nine-and-one-half.[23]
- The longer you leave funds inside the Roth after the conversion, the more time it can grow and potentially recoup the tax levied on your traditional account's withdrawals. Remember, this money is now growing tax-free. A long growth period may be able to outweigh a loss in your balance due to income tax withholdings at conversion time. Also, an error in estimates of future tax rate margins (i.e., your future rates turned out to be less than the conversion year) can be made up by holding funds in your Roth for many years.[24]
- Planning to use your Roth as a legacy planning tool? There are various rules and options depending on the

---

[23] Kailey Hagen. The Motley Fool. November 16, 2022. "4 Things to Know If You're Considering a Roth IRA Conversion This Year" https://www.fool.com/retirement/2022/11/16/4-things-to-know-if-youre-considering-a-roth-ira-c/

[24] Tim Steffen. Baird Wealth. October 16, 2023. "The Three Tests Before a Roth Conversion" https://www.bairdwealth.com/insights/wealth-management-perspectives/2023/09/the-three-tests-before-a-roth-conversion/

type of heir, but in most cases the Roth is given additional time to grow tax-free.

Does that make your head spin? Understandable. That's why it's so important to work with a financial professional and tax planner who can help you execute these sorts of tax-efficient strategies and help you understand what you are doing and why. A tax strategy created by a financial planner who partners with a tax professional is going to be one that will instill confidence. A tax strategy curated by experts will feel like someone is holding your hand as you plan for and approach retirement.

CHAPTER 3

Market Volatility

Up and down. Roller coaster. Merry-go-round. Bulls and bears. Peak-to-trough.

Sound familiar? This is the language we use to talk about the stock market. With volatility and spikes, even our language is jarring, bracing, and vivid.

Still, financial strategies tend to revolve around market-based products, and for good reasons. For one thing, there is no other financial class that packs the same potential for growth, pound for pound, as stock-based products. Because of growth potential, inflation challenges, and new opportunities, it may be unwise to avoid the market entirely.

However, along with the potential for growth is the potential for loss. At the time this book was written, many of the people I've seen in my office came in feeling uneasy because of the economic fallout of the COVID-19 outbreak of 2020, followed by the economic downturn and the inflation spike that happened in 2022.

So, how do we balance these factors? How do we try to satisfy both the need for protection and the need for growth?

For one thing, it is important to recognize the value of diversity. Now, I'm not just talking about the diversity of assets among different kinds of stocks, or even different kinds of stocks and bonds. That's only one kind of diversity. Stocks and bonds, though different, are both still important market-based products. Even within a diverse portfolio, most market-based products tend to rise or fall as a whole, just like an incoming tide. Therefore, a portfolio diverse in only market-sourced products won't automatically preserve your assets during times when the market declines.

In addition to the sort of "horizontal diversity" you have by purchasing a variety of stocks and bonds from different companies, I also suggest you think about "vertical diversity," or diversity among asset classes. This means having different product types, including securities products, bank products, and insurance products — with varying levels of growth potential, liquidity, and protection — all in accordance with your unique situation, goals, and needs.

Our action plan looks at your risk tolerance and how you react to market volatility. The process we go through to develop the plan uses questions and analysis to determine your philosophy on market-based risk. For example, how did you react to the dot.com bubble during the early 2000s? How did you cope with the 2008 Great Recession? What did you do right during those periods of volatility? We then use technology to help us determine where you are in terms of your portfolio balance and where you should be.

In many cases, a person's risk tolerance assessment does not align with our assessment. A client might describe their risk tolerance as moderate, but our technology finds their investment profile to be aggressive. In that case, we would go back to the client and let them know that their portfolio is currently aggressively balanced, and they might want to consider changes to align more with their risk profile.

You should be comfortable with your position regarding risk because fear leads to bad investing decisions. For example, in 2008, the S&P 500® was down 37 percent.[25] That was unprecedented. We hadn't had a crash like that in quite some time. People's 401((k)s were wiped out overnight. People panicked and sold assets locking in that loss. Rather than ride

---

[25] Jonathan Heller. Real Money. September 26, 2022. "When It Comes to Volatility, 2022 Still Isn't 2008... Yet."
https://realmoney.thestreet.com/investing/stocks/when-it-comes-to-volatility-2022-still-isn-t-2008-yet-16103606

the wave, they were so scared that they sold and took the loss of 37 percent. In 2009, the market picked up and it was a good year by anybody's standards. The returns were roughly 20 percent. Despite that, people were so shell-shocked that the market could correct again. People would not go back into the market.

The next year, 2010, was another great year. Investopedia reports returns were about 15 percent.[26] So, we had two great years following a horrible year in 2008. Still, most people who were of retirement age were out of the market because they were afraid they would miss the return. Some people started to come back into the market in 2010, but the damage was already done. If you were turning sixty-five in 2008, your retirement changed significantly. You couldn't retire potentially, or you needed to work until you were seventy. If your employer wouldn't keep you until you were seventy, you had to take a job that paid less. Some joke that the Walmart greeter came from that time period because so many people needed additional income because they couldn't quite retire.

So, the scary part of market volatility is that without a plan, you could find yourself having to accept a lower standard of living. Most importantly, the closer you get to retirement, the more you have to be mindful of market volatility because you don't have time to make up for any losses. Advisors call it the sequence of returns risk, which basically translates to market timing. You can't really control what the market's going to do when you decide to retire. If there have been multiple down years in a row before you retire, your retirement income could be crushed if you haven't planned correctly. You need things in place and some time to mitigate the volatility on a portion of your assets. You still have a portion of your assets that create income while your market-based assets recover.

---

[26] J.B. Maverick. Investopedia. May 24, 2023. "S&P 500. Average Return." https://www.investopedia.com/ask/answers/042415/what-average-annual-return-sp-500.asp

The Color of Money

When you're looking at the overall diversity of your portfolio, part of the equation is knowing which products fit in what category: what has liquidity, what has asset preservation, and what has growth potential.

Before we dive in, keep in mind these aren't absolutes. You might think of liquidity, growth, and asset preservation as primary colors. While some products will look pretty much yellow, red, or blue, others will have a mix of characteristics, making them more green, orange, or purple.

Growth

I like to think of the growth category as red. It's powerful, it's somewhat volatile, and it's also the category where we have the greatest opportunities for growth and loss. Often, products in the growth category will have a good deal of liquidity but very little protection. These are our market-based products and strategies, and we think of them mostly in shades of red and orange to designate their growth and liquidity. This is usually a good place to be when you're young — think fast cars and flashy leather jackets — but its allure often wanes as you move closer to retirement. Examples of "red" products include:

- Stocks
- Equities
- Exchange-traded funds
- Mutual funds
- Corporate bonds
- Real estate investment trusts
- Speculations
- Alternative investments

Liquidity

Yellow is my liquid category color. I typically recommend having at least enough yellow money to cover six months' to a year's worth of expenses in case of emergency. Yellow assets don't need a lot of growth potential; they just need to be readily available when we need them. The "yellow" category includes assets like:

- Cash
- Money market accounts

Asset Preservation

The color of asset preservation, to me, is blue, which can incorporate products such as annuities. Tranquil, sure — even if it lacks a certain amount of flash. This is the direction I like to see people generally move toward as they're nearing retirement. The red, flashy look of stock market returns and the risk of possible overnight losses are less attractive as we near retirement and look for more consistency and reliability. While this category doesn't come with a lot of liquidity, the products here are backed by an insurance company, a bank, or a government entity. "Blue" products include things such as:

- Certificates of deposit (backed by banks)
- Government-based bonds (backed by the U.S. government)
- Life insurance (backed by insurance companies)
- Annuities (backed by insurance companies)

Planners may use many different types of asset classes in a holistic portfolio, including CDs, government bonds, life insurance, and annuities. The reason is to create some certainties around money in retirement, reduce risk, but not sacrifice the opportunity for growth. You want to have your cake and eat it too. These market-based products do that for you. For example, if you use life insurance, you benefit from some unique tax advantages. Annuities guarantee income. If you want to have a pension plan but your work doesn't provide one, an annuity is similar to a personal pension and can give you guaranteed income for life. Somebody who is incredibly market-adverse might like an annuity because there's a lot of inherent guarantees built in. That might relieve some anxiety regarding potential market losses. The rule of 4 percent says that you should not spend more than 4 percent of your assets. So, if you had a million dollars and you wanted it to last forever, you can only take 4 percent per year. We use these products because many pay better than 4 percent. For example, an annuity might pay 6 percent, which is better because it's a guaranteed increase of 2 percent.

The assets are really designed to protect the downside so that when a 2008 year comes, you have a portion of your assets that can withstand the volatility and drive income. Let's say 70 or 80 percent of your assets that are not in those vehicles are going to recover from the rollercoaster ride of the market, you may have some income, protection, and liquidity. You won't have to pull from your already depleted market-based assets.

401(k)s

I want to take a second to specifically address a product many retirees will be using to build their retirement income: the 401(k) and other retirement accounts. Any of these retirement accounts (IRAs, 401(k)s, 403(b)s, etc.) are basically "tax wrappers." What do I mean by that? Well, depending on your plan provider, a 401(k) could include target-date funds, passively managed products, stocks, bonds, mutual funds, or even variable, fixed, and fixed index annuities, all collected in one place and governed by rules (a.k.a. the "tax wrapper"). These rules govern how much money you can put inside, what ways you can put it in, when you will pay taxes on it, and when you can take the money out. Inside the 401(k), each of the products inside the "tax wrapper" might have its own fees or commissions, in addition to the management fee you pay on the 401(k) itself.

Now, fees can be troublesome. You can't get something for nothing, and fees are how many financial companies and professionals make a living. Yet, it's important to recognize even a fee with a fraction of a percentage point is money out of your pocket — money that represents not just the one-time fee of today but also an opportunity cost. For example, consider how a $100,000 IRA that earns 6 percent over a twenty-five-year period without investment fees would earn $430,000. But if just a 0.5 percent fee was factored into that investment, the IRA would be worth $379,000 in twenty-five years — a $50,500 decrease. For someone close to retirement, how much do you think fees may have cost over their lifetime?

Even for those close to retirement, it's important to look at management fees and assess if you think you're getting what you pay for. Over the course of ten years, those costs can add up, and you may have decades ahead of you in which you will need to rely on your assets.

Dollar-Cost Averaging

With 401(k)s and other market-based retirement products, dollar-cost averaging is a concept that can work in your favor when you are investing for the long term. When the market is trending up, if you are consistently paying in money, month over month, great; your investments can grow, and you are adding to your assets. When the market takes a dip, no problem; your dollars buy more shares at a lower price. At some point, we hope the market will rebound, in which case your shares can grow and possibly be more valuable than they were before. This concept is what we call "dollar-cost averaging." While it can't ensure a profit or guarantee against losses, it's a time-tested strategy for investing in a volatile market.

However, when you are in retirement, this strategy may work against you. You may have heard of "reverse" dollar-cost averaging. Before, when the market lost ground, you were "bargain-shopping"; your dollars purchased more assets at a reduced price. When you are in retirement, you are no longer the purchaser; you are selling. So, in a down market, you have to sell more assets to make the same amount of money as what you made in a favorable market.

I've had lots of people step into my office to talk to me about this, emphasizing how their advisor says, "the market always bounces back, and I have to just hold on for the long term."

There's some basis for this thinking; thus far, the market has always rebounded to higher heights than before. But this is no guarantee, and the prospect of potentially higher returns in five years may not be very helpful in retirement if you are relying on the income from those returns to pay this month's electric bill, for example.

We diversify your assets from a tax perspective. We do this by choosing assets carefully and incorporating products that give the client peace of mind, such as an annuity that provides guaranteed future income and life insurance that replaces income if somebody passes away. These products can be the building block for all your other investments. If we can derive a baseline income from an annuity and insure against lost income in the event of a death, we can have a better conversation about next steps. The conversation includes a discussion of how much risk we can take now that we know that a certain percentage of your retirement income is guaranteed. With annuities and life insurance as the foundational components, we can start to layer on the other pieces.

Is There a "Perfect" Product?

To bring us back around to the discussion of asset preservation, growth, and liquidity, the ideal product would be a "ten" in all three categories, right? Completely guaranteed, doubling in size every few years, and accessible whenever you want. Does such a product exist? Absolutely not.

Instead of running in circles looking for that perfect product, the silver bullet, the unicorn of financial strategies, it's more important to circle back to the concept of a balanced, asset-diverse portfolio.

This is why it could be prudent to work with a knowledgeable financial professional who knows what various financial products can do and how to use them in your personal retirement strategy.*

---

* Investing involves risk, including the potential loss of principal. No investment strategy can guarantee a profit or protect against loss in periods of declining values. Any references to protection benefits or guaranteed/lifetime income streams refer only to fixed insurance products, not securities or investment products. Insurance and annuity product guarantees are backed by the financial strength and claims-paying ability of the issuing insurance company.

CHAPTER 4

Retirement Income

Retirement. For many of us, it's what we've saved for and dreamed of, pinning our hopes to a magical someday. Is that someday full of traveling? Is it filled with grandkids? Gardening? Maybe your fondest dream is simply never having to work again, never having to clock in or be accountable to someone else.

Your ability to do these things all hinges on *income*. Without the money to support these dreams, even a basic level of work-free lifestyle is unsustainable. That's why planning for your income in retirement is so foundational. But where do we begin?

It's easy to feel overwhelmed by this question. Some may feel the urge to amass a large lump sum and then try to put it all in one product — insurance, investments, liquid assets — to provide all the growth, liquidity, and income they need. Instead, I think you need a more balanced approach. After all, retirement planning isn't magic. As I mention elsewhere, there is no single product that can be all things to all people (or even all things to one person). No approach works unilaterally for everyone. That's why it's important to talk to a financial professional who can help you lay down the basics and take you step-by-step through the process. Not only will you have the assurance you have addressed the areas you need to, but you will also have an ally who can help you break down the process and help keep you from feeling overwhelmed.

Sources of Income

Thinking of all the pieces of your retirement expenses might be intimidating. But, like cleaning out a junk drawer or revisiting that garage remodel, once you have laid everything out, you can begin to sort things into categories.

Once you have a good overall picture of where your expenses will lie, you can start stacking up the resources to cover them.

Social Security

Social Security is a guaranteed, inflation-adjusted federal insurance program that plays a significant part in most of our retirement plans. From delaying until you've reached full retirement age or beyond to examining spousal benefits, as I discuss elsewhere in this book, there is plenty you can do to try to make the most of this monthly benefit. As with all your retirement income sources, it's important to consider ways to make this resource stretch to provide the most bang and buck for your situation.

Pension

Another generally reliable source of retirement income for you might be a pension, if you are one of the lucky people who still has one.

If you don't have a pension, go ahead and skim on to the next section. If you do have a pension, keep on reading.

Because your pension can be such a central piece of your retirement income plan, you will want to put some thought into answering basic questions about it.

How well is your pension funded? Since the heyday of the pension plan, companies and governments have neglected to fund their pension obligations, causing a persistent problem with this otherwise reliable asset.

Consider the factors at play, though. Pensions had been underfunded and gained a boost from strong market performance, most recently in 2021.[27] What happens to the solvency of those pension funds if the market declines?

It can be worthwhile to keep tabs on your pension's health and know what your options are for withdrawing from it. Typically, you have one chance at electing the distribution option at your retirement with no recourse to change at a later date, so you will want to look at all options before making a final decision. If you have already retired and made those decisions, this may be a foregone conclusion. If not, it pays to know what you can expect and what decisions you can make, such as taking spousal options to cover your spouse if they outlive you.

Also, some companies are incentivizing lump-sum payouts of pensions to reduce the companies' payment liabilities. If that's the case with your employer, talk to your financial professional to see if it might be prudent to do something like that or if it might be better to stick with lifetime payments or other options.

Your 401(k) and IRA

One "modern way" to save for retirement is in a 401(k) or IRA (or their nonprofit or governmental equivalents). These tax-advantaged accounts are, in my opinion, a poor substitute for pensions, but one of the biggest disservices we do to ourselves is not taking full advantage of them in the first place. While the average 401(k) balance for Americans between the ages of forty and forty-nine is $105,500, the median account balance is

---

[27] pewtrusts.org. November 8, 2023. "Public Retirement Systems Need Sustainable Policies to Navigate Volatile Financial Markets" https://www.pewtrusts.org/en/research-and-analysis/issue-briefs/2023/11/public-retirement-systems-need-sustainable-policies-to-navigate-volatile-financial-markets

much lower. The median, which separates half of accounts with higher balances and half with lower balances, is just $34,100.[28]

Also, if you have changed jobs over the years, do the work of tracking down any benefits from your past employers. You might have an IRA here or a 401(k) there; keep track of those so you can pull them together and look at those assets when you're ready to look at establishing sources of retirement income.

Do You Have ...

- Life insurance?
- Annuities?
- Long-term care insurance?
- Any passive income sources?
- Stock and bond portfolios?
- Liquid assets? (What's in your bank account?)
- Alternative investments?
- Rental properties?

If you are going through the work of sitting with a financial professional, it's important to look at your full retirement income picture and pull together *all* your assets, no matter how big or small. From the free insurance policy offered at your bank to the sizable investment in your brother-in-law's modestly successful furniture store, you want to have a good idea of where your money is.

Joe and Donna became clients after attending one of our seminars. Joe worked for the local township, and Donna worked for a large Fortune 500 company for almost her whole career. They lived in a mid-to-upper-class town in New Jersey in a modest house. Still, it was expensive to live there. The couple also had three children that they put through college.

---

[28] Cheyenne DeVon. cnbc.com. July 13, 2023. "Here's how much Americans in their 40s have in their 401(k)s"
https://www.cnbc.com/2023/07/13/fidelity-how-much-americans-in-their-40s-have-in-their-401ks.html

The couple was committed to saving and were among the best savers I've ever seen, and they had never done any formal planning. They just saved because they knew they wanted to retire without a problem when the time came. They also knew that Joe would receive a pension from his job with the township.

A pension is a significant foundational piece of getting to retirement. If you have a pension, you may be ahead of the game. Joe had his pension, Donna had been working for the same company for approximately thirty years. They brown-bagged lunch, and sacrificed to make sure they hit their retirement dream. However, they had no idea what that dream would cost. They had no idea how much they had saved and what those funds would equate to. We sat down with them and went through our process. As we learned more about them, we realized that they had done a tremendous job of saving, but they couldn't see it.

In retirement, Joe and Donna wanted to spend part of the year in Florida and part of the year in Cape Cod. There were expenses to that, including a car and somewhere to stay in both places. We brainstormed their expenses to get some idea of how much income they would need to live the lifestyle they envisioned.

Next, we plugged all of their assets into our modeling software to find how much income they would have when they retired and if that would be enough.

"You're going to have something in the neighborhood of $17,000," I told them.

Donna started to cry.

"You're telling us that all that hard work has only given us $17,000 a year? What can we do with that?" she asked.

"No, Donna," I said, "That's $17,000 a month."

At that news, she started to cry even harder. Because of their savings, Joe and Donna were going to earn more in retirement than they currently earned working. They were going to get a pay raise to retire. They would have zero debt, their two houses would be paid off, and they would have $17,000 a month to spend. The couple both decided to retire immediately or as soon as they could process the paperwork.

Retirement Income Needs

How much income will you need in retirement? How do you determine that? A lot of people work toward a random number, thinking, "If I can just have a million dollars, I'll be comfortable in retirement!" Don't get me wrong; it is possible to save up a lot of money and then retire in the hopes you can keep your monthly expenses lower than some set estimation. But I think this carries a general risk of running out of money. Instead, I work with my clients to find out what their current and projected income needs are and then work from there to see how we might cover any gaps between what they have and what they want.

Goals and Dreams

I like to start with your pie in the sky. Do you find yourself planning for your vacations more thoroughly than you do your retirement? Maybe it's because planning a vacation is less stressful: Having a week at the beach go awry is, well, a walk on the beach compared to running out of money in retirement. Whatever the case, perhaps it would be better if you thought of your retirement as a vacation in and of itself — no clocking in, no boss, no overtime. If you felt unlimited by financial strain, what would you do?

Would an endless vacation for you mean Paris and Rome? Would it mean mentoring at children's clubs or serving at the local soup kitchen? Or maybe it would mean deepening your ties to those immediately around you — neighbors, friends, and family. Maybe it would mean more time to take part in the hobbies and activities you love. Have you been considering a second (or even third) act as a small-business owner, turning a hobby or passion into a revenue source?

This is your time to daydream and answer the question: If you could do anything, what would you do?

After that, it's a matter of putting a dollar amount on it. What are the costs of round-the-world travel? One couple I know said their highest priority in retirement was being able to take each of their grandchildren on a cross-country vacation every year. That's a pretty specific goal — one that is reasonably easy to nail down a budget for.

I ask my seminar attendees to fill out a feedback form when they first arrive. The form asks questions, such as, "What are your biggest concerns regarding retirement? Are you most worried about running out of money, long-term care, making poor choices, or not being able to leave a legacy?" But the most important question is, "What is your retirement goal?"

Most people have a goal, but they never realize it because they are too fearful to try. They can articulate what they want to do, but they never actually do it because they are too scared they will run out of money if they do. If a plan is there, and if the numbers are clear about what happens from age seventy-five to eighty and then from age eighty to eighty-five, the dreams become reality because clients are confident they can afford the lifestyle they want.

Current Budget

Compiling a current expense report is one of the trickiest pieces of retirement preparation. Many people assume the expenses of their lives in retirement will be lower. After all, there will be no drive to work, no need for a formal wardrobe, and — perhaps most impactful of all — no more saving for retirement!

Yet, we often underestimate our daily spending habits. That's why I typically ask my clients to bring in their bank statements for the past year — they are reflective of your *actual* spending, not just what you think you're spending.

We do have some clients who are pre-retirees and confident they know how much they will need in retirement. For those clients, we still run through our three-step process. We look at their current household spending and consider how that might change in the next five or six years. For example, they might still be semi-supporting an older child. We set up a model as best we can and determine if a client's spending is up to or below their means. Many people actually spend below their means.

This process helps us build a baseline for their future income needs based on how they want to approach retirement. We call the first ten years of retirement the go-go years, the next ten are the slow-go years, and the last ten are the no-go years. You need more money for the earlier years because you are healthy, ambitious, you're no longer working, and you have some money and want to spend it. As time goes by, some people slow down their spending until they really are not spending much at all, comparatively. My father is eighty, and he spends just a fraction of the money he spent thirty years ago.

Fundamentally, we find a baseline that gives you the confidence to spend your money on your goals and dreams.

I can't count the number of times I have sat with a couple, asked them about their spending, and heard them throw out a number that seemed incredibly low. When I ask them where the number came from, they usually say they estimated based on their total bills. Yet, our spending is so much more than our mortgage, utilities, cable, phone, car, grocery, or credit card bills.

"What about clothes?" I ask, "Or dining out? What about gifts and coffees and last-minute birthday cards?" That's when the lights come on.

This is why I suggest collecting a year's worth of information. There is usually no such thing as a one-time purchase. Did you buy new furniture? Even if that is a rarity, do you think that will be the last time you *ever* buy furniture?

One client, I remember, had a budget that shocked me. I was not sure I could manage to get him where he wanted to be in his retirement because his expenses were so high. He was a doctor and a high-income earner. He had three daughters who were all in school studying for a master's or PhD, and my client was funding their graduate studies. My client also wanted to pay for their houses and their cars, and he was also looking to retire in the next two to five years.

To run his household, he needed something like $650,000 a year after tax. Also, he had an incredibly conservative mindset and was fearful of the market. I looked at his position and although he was worth a significant amount of money, I was not sure I could get him to $650,000 after tax and support that for the rest of his life. We could set him up for ten years, but I wasn't sure we could make that work for the next twenty years. This was a unique situation. We had significant net worth, money in the bank, but because of what he was spending and the way he viewed the market, we had some challenges. Ultimately, we were able to create a plan to meet his needs.

Another hefty expense is spending on the kids. Many of the couples I work with are quick to help their adult children, whether it's something like letting them live in the basement, paying for college, babysitting, paying an occasional bill, or contributing to a grandchild's college fund. Research concluded that 54 percent of those in the Gen Z and millennial age groups lean on parents for financial support. Among those, 23 percent are heavily supported by parents.[29]

My clients sometimes protest that what they do for their grown children can stop in retirement. They don't *need* to help. But I get it. Parents like to feel needed. And, while you never want to neglect saving for retirement in favor of taking on financial risks (like your child's student debt), the parents who help their adult children do so in part because it helps them feel fulfilled.

When it comes down to expenses, including (and especially) spending on your family, don't make your initial calculations based on what you *could* whittle your budget down to if you *had*

---

[29] Experianpic.com. June 27, 2023. "Most Gen Zers and millennials still rely on parents for financial support and feel ashamed asking for help" https://www.experianplc.com/newsroom/press-releases/2023/most-gen-zers-and-millennials-still-rely-on-parents-for-financial-support-and-feel-ashamed-asking-for-help

to. Instead, start from where you are. Who wants to live off a bare-bones bank account in retirement?

Other Expenses

Once you have nailed down your current budget and your dreams or goals for retirement, there are a few other outstanding pieces to think about — some expenses many people don't take the time to consider before making and executing a plan. But I'm assuming you want to get it right, so let's take a look.

Housing

Do you know where you want to live in retirement? This makes up a substantial piece of your income puzzle — since the typical American household owns a home, and it's generally their largest asset.

Some people prefer to live right where they are for as long as they can. Others have been waiting for retirement to pull the trigger on an ambitious move, like purchasing a new house, or even downsizing. Whatever your plans and whatever your reasons, there are quite a few things to consider.

Mortgage

Do you still have a mortgage? What may have been a nice tax boon in your working years could turn into a financial burden in your retirement. After all, when you are on a limited income, a mortgage is just one more bill sapping your financial strength. It is something to put some thought into, whether you plan to age in place or are considering moving to your dream home, buying a house out of state, or living in a retirement community.

Upkeep and Taxes

A house without a mortgage still requires annual taxes. While it's tempting to think of this as a once-a-year expense, when you have limited earning potential, your annual tax bill might be something into which you should put a little more forethought.

The costs of homeownership aren't just monetary. When you find yourself dealing with more house than you need, it can drain your time and energy. From keeping clutter at bay to keeping the lawn mower running, upkeep can be extensive and expensive. For some, that's a challenge they heartily accept and can comfortably take on. For others, the idea of yard work or cleaning an area larger than they need feels foolish.

For instance, Peggy discovered after her knee replacement that most of her house was inaccessible to her when she was laid up.

"It felt ridiculous to pay someone else to dust and vacuum a house I was only living in 40 percent of!"

Practicality and Adaptability

Erik and Marla are looking to retire within the next two decades. They just sold their old three-bedroom ranch-style house. Their twins are in high school, and the couple has wanted to "upgrade" for years. Now they live in a gorgeous 1940s three-story house with all the kitchen space they ever wanted, five sprawling bedrooms, and a library and media room for themselves and their children. Within months of moving in, the couple realized a house perfect for their active teens would no longer be perfect for them in five to fifteen years.

"We are paying the mortgage for this house, but we've started saving for the next one," said Marla, "because who wants to climb two flights of stairs to their bedroom when they're seventy-eight?"

Others I know have encountered a similar situation in their personal lives. After a health crisis, one couple found the luxurious tub for two they toiled to install had become a specter of a bad slip and a potential safety risk. It's important to think through what your physical reality could be. I always emphasize to my clients that they should plan for whatever their long-term future might hold, but it's amazing how many people don't give it much thought.

Contracts and Regulations

If you are looking into a cross-country move, be aware of new tax tables or local ordinances in the area where you are looking to move. After all, you don't want to experience sticker-shock when you are looking at downsizing or reducing your bills in retirement.

Along the same lines, if you are moving into a retirement community, be sure to look at the fine print. What happens if you must move into a different situation for long-term care? Will you be penalized? Will you be responsible for replacing your slot in the community? What are all the fees, and what do they cover?

Inflation

As I write this in 2024, America has experienced a wave of inflation following a lengthy period of low inflation. Inflation zoomed to 9.1 percent in June 2022, its highest mark since November 1981.[30] By the end of 2023, the inflation rate decreased to 3.1 percent.[31]

Core inflation is yet another measurement that excludes goods with prices that tend to be more volatile, such as food and energy costs. Core inflation for a twelve-month period ending

---

[30] tradingeconomics.com. 2022 Data/2023 Forecast/1914-2021 Historical. "United States Inflation Rate" https://tradingeconomics.com/united-states/inflation-cpi

[31] statistica.com. December 13, 2023. "Monthly 12-month inflation rate in the United States from November 2020 to November 2023" https://www.statista.com/statistics/273418/unadjusted-monthly-inflation-rate-in-the-us

in November 2023 was 4.0 percent. It so happened that energy prices decreased 5.4 percent over that timeframe.[32]

However, inflation isn't a one-time bump; it has a cumulative effect. Again, that can impact the price of groceries more than other goods. Even with relatively low inflation over the past few decades, an item you bought in 1997 for $2 will cost about $4.35 today.[33] Want to go to a show? A $20 ticket in 1997 would cost $43.50 in 2023.[34]

What if we hit a stretch in retirement like the late seventies and early eighties, when annual inflation rates of 10 percent became the norm? It may be wise to consider some extra padding in your retirement income plan to account for any potential increase in inflation in the future.

Shrinkflation

Another important yet often overlooked factor to consider is called "shrinkflation." Essentially a form of hidden inflation, shrinkflation signifies a reduction in packaging while retaining a similar price as before.

For example, as you walk down a grocery store aisle, you spot your favorite pickles. The jar still costs the same — roughly $5 — and you add it to your cart. Then you get home, and the container seems different after digging out a few crispy dills. You examine the jar and discover it contains fewer ounces than previous jars you purchased. However, you paid roughly the same price for your pickles.

Now, move over to the aisle featuring salty snacks. You might notice a sale on a certain brand of chips, though you must buy

---

[32] U.S. Inflation Calculator. "United States Core Inflation Rates (1957-2022)" https://www.usinflationcalculator.com/inflation/united-states-core-inflation-rates/
[33] In2013dollars.com. "$2 in 1997 is worth $3.70 today" https://www.in2013dollars.com/us/inflation/1997?amount=2
[34] In2013dollars.com "Admission to movies, theaters, and concerts priced at $20 in 1997>$40.34 in 2022" https://www.in2013dollars.com/Admission-to-movies,-theaters,-and-concerts/price-inflation

three or four bags to receive a discount promoted by the store. You decide to purchase that many bags to capitalize on the lower price. When you get home, you notice the packaging is smaller than you anticipated. The deal you accepted may not have been as thrifty as you perceived.

Shrinkflation can be a way for companies to quietly boost, or retain, profit margins without having to change much else — essentially, they are simply charging the same price for less product. Companies do this because customers are more likely to spot price increases than size reductions. However, research has also shown that these shrinkflation tactics can backfire into negative consumer perceptions of their brands once they come to light. Who wants to pay the same for less, especially when they have already grown accustomed to getting more for their money's worth?[35]

Aging

Also, in the expense category, think about longevity. We all hope to age gracefully. However, it's important to face the prospect of aging with a sense of realism.

For many families, the elephant in the room is long-term care. No one wants to admit they will likely need it, but estimates indicate almost 70 percent of us will.[36] Aging is a significant piece of retirement income planning because you'll want to figure out how to set aside money for your care, either at home or away from it. The more comfortable you get with discussing your wishes and plans with your loved ones, the easier planning for the financial side of it can be.

I denote health care and potential long-term care costs in more detail elsewhere in this book, but suffice it to say nursing

---

[35] Daniel Liberto. Investopedia. November 16, 2023. "Shrinkflation: What It Is, Reasons for It, How to Spot It"
https://www.investopedia.com/terms/s/shrinkflation.asp
[36] Moll Law Group. 2022. "The Cost of Long-Term Care"
https://www.molllawgroup.com/the-cost-of-long-term-care.html

home care tends to be very expensive and typically isn't something you get to choose when you will need.

It isn't just the costs of long-term care that pose a concern in living longer. It's also about covering the possible costs of everything else associated with living longer. For instance, if Henry retires from his job as a biochemical engineer at age sixty-five, perhaps he plans to have a very decent income for twenty years until he turns eighty-five. But what if he lives until he's ninety-five? That's a whole third — ten years — more of personal income he will need.

Putting It All Together

Whew! So, you have pulled together what you have, and you have a pretty good idea of where you want to be. Now, you and your financial professional can go about the work of arranging what assets you *have* to cover what you *need* — and how you might try to cover any gaps.

Like the proverbial man in the Bible who built his house on a rock, I like to help my clients figure out how to cover their day-to-day living expenses — their needs — with insurance and other guaranteed income sources like pensions and Social Security.

Deciding whether a couple can retire is really a fact-finding process and also a process of getting to know the client on a personal level. We need to know if they have goals and what those goals are. We need to know what assets they have and put the assets down on paper to create what we call our action plan.

Our action plan is a roadmap that helps clients envisage what their retirement could look like based on their assets and goals. It's a thorough process and usually takes a few meetings. The first meeting is usually to gather information, and the remaining meetings are spent determining what to do with the information we're given and to find out if we can meet a client's expectations or, ideally, exceed them. It's a systematic, process-driven process because we have to make sure we gather all the information so that our assumptions are accurate.

Again, you should keep in mind there isn't one single financial vehicle, asset, or source to fill all your needs, and that's okay. One of the challenges of planning for your income in retirement concerns figuring out what products and strategies to use. You can release some of that stress when you accept the fact you will probably need a diverse portfolio — potentially with bonds, stocks, insurance, and other income sources — not just one massive money pile.

One way to help shore up your income gaps is by working with your financial professional and a qualified tax advisor to help mitigate your tax exposure. If you have a 401(k) or IRA, a tax advisor in your corner may be able to help you figure out how and when to take distributions from your account in a way that doesn't push you into a higher tax bracket. Or you might learn ways to use tax-advantaged bonds more effectively. Effective tax planning isn't necessarily about "adding" to your income. Especially regarding retirement, it's less about what you make than it is about what you keep. Paying a lower tax bill keeps more money in your pocket, which is where you want it when it comes to retirement income.

Now you can look at ways to cover your remaining retirement goals. Are there products like long-term care insurance specific to a certain kind of expense you anticipate? Is there a particular asset you want to use for your "play" money — money for trips and gifts for the grandkids? Is there any way you can portion off money for those charitable legacy plans?

Once you have analyzed your income wants, needs, and the assets necessary to realistically cover them, you may have a gap. The masterstroke of a competent financial professional will be to help you figure out how you will cover that gap. Will you need to cut out a round of golf a week? Maybe skip the new car? Or will you need to take more substantial action?

One way to cover an income gap is to consider working longer or even part-time before retirement and even after that magical calendar date. This may not be the best "plan" for you;

disabilities, work demands, and physical or emotional limitations can hinder the best-laid plans to continue working. However, if it is physically possible for you, this is one considerable way to help your assets last for more than one reason.

In fact, 55 percent of the Americans responding to a survey report they plan to work part-time after retiring, while 15 percent expect compensation from work to be their primary source of retirement income.[37]

The process we use to plan should be a freeing experience. If we do it right, the client learns a lot about their financial situation. Ideally, at the end of it, we can tell the client exactly when they can retire. I grew up in close proximity to New York in a commuter town that was home to many Wall Street executives. I have worked with many finance executives because I understood who they were, how they operate, how they get paid, that sort of thing. I mentioned this before, but for these executives, the tap on the shoulder is never far away when they reach age fifty-five because they're just too expensive to keep on board. So, when they reach their mid-to-late fifties, they start looking for a package to retire.

Mike was a client who worked for a large, prominent bank. He was a little bit older than the average executive, and he knew what he wanted in retirement. He told me that he wanted to live for two years in a penthouse in New York City with his wife Rita. That had always been an unrealized dream for them. Mike and Rita's ultimate goal was to then move to southern California and retire there. That's the opposite of what most people do when they retire. Most people leave California when they retire because the taxes are so high.

We put Mike and Rita through our process and mapped out the expected costs of a penthouse in New York City and then a move to California. We factored in the fact that Mike would

---

[37] Kerry Hannon. Yahoo!finance.com. July 15, 2023. "Future retirees plan to work longer, partly due to savings shortfalls"
https://finance.yahoo.com/news/future-retirees-plan-to-work-longer-partly-due-to-savings-shortfalls-160038419.html

have to look for a new job in California because he couldn't transfer from the bank where he was currently employed. We were able to show the couple, on paper, that they could take action on their retirement dream. Five years later, Mike and Rita are thriving. Mike actually landed a job close to home making more money than he ever made before. He didn't necessarily need to go back to work in that capacity, but he is living his dream in California and couldn't be happier.

When you're retired, you no longer have an employer paying you a steady check. It is up to you to make sure you have saved and planned for the income you need.

CHAPTER 5

Social Security

Social Security is often the foundation of retirement income. Backed by the strength of the U.S. Treasury, it provides perhaps the most dependable paycheck you will have in retirement.

From the time you collect your first paycheck from the job that made you a bona fide taxpayer, you are paying into the grand old Social Security system. My first job was with a company called Thrifty Car Rental. I worked for Thrifty based inside of a Texaco gas station in Summit, New Jersey. I have fond memories of that job because that gas station was in the center of the town I grew up in. All my friends and anyone who knew me would stop by to say hello.

What grew and developed out of the pressures of the Great Depression has become one of the most popular government programs in the country, and if you pay in for the equivalent of ten years or more, you, too, can benefit from the Social Security program.

Now, before we get into the nitty gritty of Social Security, I'd like to address a current concern: Will Social Security still be there for you when you reach retirement age?

The Future of Social Security

This question is ever-present as headlines trumpet an underfunded Social Security program, alongside the sea of baby boomers retiring in droves and the comparatively smaller pool of younger people who are funding the system.

The Social Security Administration itself acknowledges this concern as each Social Security statement now contains a link to its website (ssa.gov) and a page entitled, "Will Social Security Be There For Me?"

Just a reminder, as if you needed one, that nothing in life is guaranteed. Additionally, depending on who you're listening to, Social Security funds may run low before 2034, thanks to the financial instability and government spending that accompanied the 2020 COVID-19 pandemic.

Before you get too discouraged, though, here are a few thoughts to keep you going:

- Even if the program is only paying 75-78 cents on the dollar for scheduled benefits, this is notably not zero.
- The Social Security Administration has made changes in the distant and near past to help protect the fund's solvency, including increasing retirement ages and striking certain filing strategies.
- There are many changes Congress could make, and lawmakers routinely discuss ideas for amending the system, such as further increasing full retirement age and eligibility.
- One thing no one is seriously discussing? Reneging on current obligations to retirees or the soon-to-retire.

Take heart. The real answer to the question, "Will Social Security be there for me?" is still yes.

This question is important to consider when you look at how much we, as a nation, rely on this program. Did you know Social Security benefits replace about 40 percent of a person's original income when they retire?[38]

---

[38] ssa.gov. "Alternate Measure of Replacement Rates for Social Security Benefits and Retirement Income" https://www.ssa.gov/policy/docs/ssb/v68n2/v68n2p1.html.

If you ask me, that's a pretty significant piece of your retirement income puzzle.

Another caveat? You may not realize this, but no one can legally "advise" you about your Social Security benefits.

"But, Matt," you may be thinking, "isn't that part of what you do? And what about that nice gentleman at the Social Security Administration office I spoke with on the phone?"

Don't get me wrong. Social Security Administration employees know their stuff. They are trained to understand policies and programs, and they are usually pretty quick to tell you what you can and cannot do. But the government specifically stipulates that because Social Security is a benefit you alone have paid into and earned. Your Social Security decisions are *also* yours alone.

When it comes to financial professionals, we can't push you in any direction, but — there's a big but here — working with a well-informed financial professional is still incredibly handy for your Social Security decisions. Why? Because someone who's worth their salt will know what withdrawal strategies might pertain to your specific situation and will ask questions that can help you determine what you are looking for when it comes to your Social Security.

For instance, some people want the highest possible monthly benefit. Others want to start their benefits early, and not always because of financial need. I heard about one man who called in to start his Social Security payments the day he qualified just because he liked to think of it as the government paying back a debt it owed him, and he enjoyed the feeling of receiving a check from Uncle Sam.

Whatever your reasons, questions, or feelings regarding Social Security, the decision is yours alone, but working with a financial professional can help you put your options in perspective by showing you — both with industry knowledge and with proprietary software or planning processes — where your benefits fit into your overall strategy for retirement income.

Full Retirement Age

When it comes to Social Security, it seems like many people only think so far as "yes." They don't take the time to understand the various options available. Instead, because it is common knowledge you can begin your benefits at age sixty-two, that's what many of us do. While more people are opting to delay taking benefits, age sixty-two is still a popular age to start.[39]

Some people fail to understand that starting benefits early may leave significant money on the table. You see, the Social Security Administration bases your monthly benefit on two factors: your earnings history and your full retirement age (FRA).

From your earnings history, the SSA pulls the thirty-five years you made the most money and uses a mathematical indexing formula to figure out a monthly average from those years. If you paid into the system for less than thirty-five years, then every year you didn't pay in will be counted as a zero.

Once they have calculated what your monthly earnings would be at FRA, the government then calculates what to put on your check based on how close you are to FRA. FRA was originally set at sixty-five, but as the population aged and lifespans lengthened, the government shifted FRA later and later, based on an individual's year of birth. Check out the following chart to see when you will reach FRA.[40]

---

[39] Emily Brandon, Erica Sandberg. U.S. News & World Report. August 14, 2023. "The Most Popular Ages to Collect Social Security" https://money.usnews.com/money/retirement/social-security/articles/the-most-popular-ages-to-collect-social-security
[40] Social Security Administration. "Full Retirement Age" https://www.ssa.gov/planners/retire/retirechart.html

Age to Receive Full Social Security Benefits*

(Called "full retirement age" [FRA] or "normal retirement age.")

Year of Birth*	FRA
1937 or earlier	65
1938	65 and 2 months
1939	65 and 4 months
1940	65 and 6 months
1941	65 and 8 months
1942	65 and 10 months
1943-1954	66
1955	66 and 2 months
1956	66 and 4 months
1957	66 and 6 months
1958	66 and 8 months
1959	66 and 10 months
1960 and later	67

*If you were born on January 1 of any year, you should refer to the previous year. (If you were born on the 1st of the month, we figure your benefit [and your full retirement age] as if your birthday was in the previous month.)[41]

When you reach FRA, you are eligible to receive 100 percent of whatever the Social Security Administration calculates as your full monthly benefit.

Starting at age sixty-two, for every year before FRA you claim benefits, your monthly check is reduced by 5 percent or more. Conversely, for every year you delay taking benefits past FRA, your monthly benefit increases by 8 percent (until age seventy — after that, there is no monetary advantage to delaying Social Security benefits). While your circumstances and needs may vary, a lot of financial professionals still urge people to at least consider delaying until they reach age seventy.

Why wait?[42]

Taking benefits early could affect your monthly check by _____.								
62	63	64	65	66	FRA 67	68	69	70
-30%	-25%	-20%	-13.3%	-6.7%	0	+8%	+16%	+24%

[43]

My Social Security

If you are over thirty, you have probably received a notice from the Social Security Administration telling you to activate something called "My Social Security." This is a handy way to learn more about your particular benefit options, keep track of your earnings record, and calculate the benefits you have accrued over the years.

Essentially, My Social Security is an online account you can activate to see your personal Social Security picture. You can

---

[41] Social Security Administration. 2023. "Normal Retirement Age" https://www.ssa.gov/oact/progdata/nra.html
[42] Social Security Administration. 2024. "Retirement Benefits" https://www.ssa.gov/pubs/EN-05-10035.pdf
[43] Social Security Administration. 2023. "Effect of Early or Delayed Retirement on Retirement Benefits" https://www.ssa.gov/oact/ProgData/ar_drc.html

access this information at www.ssa.gov/myaccount. This can be extremely helpful when it comes to planning for income in retirement and figuring out the difference between your anticipated income versus anticipated expenses.

COLA

Social Security is a largely guaranteed piece of the retirement puzzle: If you get a statement that reads you should expect $1,000 a month, you can be sure you will receive $1,000 a month. But there is one variable detail, and that is something called the cost-of-living adjustment (COLA).

The COLA is an increase in your monthly check meant to address inflation in everyday life. After all, your expenses will likely continue to experience inflation in retirement, but you will no longer have the opportunity for raises, bonuses, or promotions you had when you were working. Instead, Social Security receives an annual cost-of-living increase tied to the Department of Labor's Consumer Price Index for Urban Wage Earners and Clerical Workers (CPI-W). If the CPI-W measurement shows inflation rose a certain amount for regular goods and services, then Social Security recipients will see that reflected in their COLA.

COLA adjustments have climbed as high as 14.3 percent (1980), and in 2023, they reached 8.7 percent — the largest increase in more than forty years. In a no- or low-inflation environment (such as in 2010, 2011, and 2016), Social Security recipients will not receive an adjustment.[44] The 2024 adjustment decreased to 3.2 percent.[45] Some view the COLA as a perk, bump, or bonus, but in reality, it works more like this: Your mom sends you to the store with $2.50 for a gallon of milk. Milk costs exactly $2.50. The next week, you go back with that same amount, but it is now $2.52 for a gallon, so you go back to

---

[44] ssa.gov. "Cost-Of-Living Adjustments" ssa.gov/oact/cola/colaseries.html
[45] ssa.gov. "Cost-of-Living Adjustment (COLA) Information for 2024" https://www.ssa.gov/cola/

Mom, and she gives you 2 cents. You aren't bringing home more milk — it just costs more money.

The COLA is less about "making more money" and more about keeping seniors' purchasing power from eroding when inflation is a big factor. Still, don't let that detract from your enthusiasm about COLAs. After all, what if Mom's solution was: "Here's the same $2.50. Try to find pennies from somewhere else to get that milk!"?

Spousal Benefits

We've talked about FRA, but another big Social Security decision involves spousal benefits.

If you or your spouse has a long stretch of zeros in your earnings history — perhaps if one of you stayed home for years, caring for children or sick relatives — you may want to consider filing for spousal benefits instead of filing on your own earnings history. A spousal benefit can be up to 50 percent of the primary wage earner's benefit at full retirement age.

To begin drawing a spousal benefit, you must be at least sixty-two years old, and the primary wage earner must have already filed for their benefit. While there are penalties for taking spousal benefits early, you cannot earn credits for delaying past full retirement age.[46]

As I wrote, the spousal benefit can be a big deal for those who don't have a very long pay history, but it's important to weigh your own earned benefits against the option of withdrawing based on a fraction of your spouse's benefits.

To look at how this could play out, let's use a hypothetical couple: Mary Jane, who is sixty, and Peter, who is sixty-two.

Let's say Peter's benefit at FRA — in his case, sixty-seven — would be $1,600. If Peter begins his benefits right now (five years before FRA), his monthly check will be $1,120. If Mary Jane begins taking spousal benefits in two years at the earliest

---

[46] Social Security Administration. "Retirement Planner: Benefits For You As A Spouse" https://www.ssa.gov/planners/retire/applying6.html

date possible, her monthly benefits will be reduced to $392 per month (remember, at FRA, the most she can qualify for is half of Peter's FRA benefit).

What if Peter and Mary Jane both wait until FRA? At sixty-seven, Peter begins taking his full benefit of $1,600 a month. Two years later, when she reaches age sixty-seven, Mary Jane will qualify for $800 a month. By waiting until FRA, the couple's monthly benefit goes from $1,512 to $2,400.

What if Peter delays until age seventy to get his maximum possible benefit? For each year past FRA he delays, his monthly benefits increase by 8 percent. This means that at seventy, he could file for a monthly benefit of $1,984. However, delayed retirement credits do not affect spousal benefits, so as soon as Peter files at seventy, Mary Jane would also file (at age sixty-eight) for her maximum benefit of $800, so their highest possible combined monthly check is $2,784.[47]

When it comes to your Social Security benefits, you obviously will want to consider whether a monthly check based on a fraction of your spouse's earnings will be comparable to or larger than your own earnings history.

Divorced Spouses

There are a few considerations for those of us who have gone through a divorce. If you 1) were married for ten years or more *and* 2) have since been divorced for at least two years *and* 3) are unmarried *and* 4) your ex-spouse qualifies to begin Social Security, you qualify for a spousal benefit based on your ex-spouse's earnings history at FRA. A divorced spousal benefit is different from the married spousal benefit in one way: You

---

[47] Office of the Chief Actuary. Social Security Administration. "Social Security Benefits: Benefits for Spouses" https://www.ssa.gov/OACT/quickcalc/spouse.html#calculator

don't have to wait for your ex-spouse to file before you can file yourself.[48]

For instance, Charles and Moira were married for fifteen years before their divorce, when he was thirty-six and she was forty. Moira has been remarried for twenty years, and although Charles briefly remarried, his second marriage ended after a few years. Charles' benefits are largely calculated based on his many years of volunteering in schools, meaning his personal monthly benefit is close to zero.

Although Moira has deferred her retirement (opting to delay benefits until she is seventy), Charles can begin taking benefits calculated from Moira's work history at FRA as early as sixty-two. However, he will also have the option of waiting until FRA to collect the maximum, or 50 percent of Moira's earned monthly benefit at her FRA.

Widowed Spouses

If your marriage ended with the death of your spouse, you might claim a benefit for your spouse's earned income as their widow/widower called a survivor's benefit. Unlike spousal benefits or divorced benefits, if your spouse dies, you can claim their full benefit. Also, unlike spousal benefits, you can begin taking income when you turn sixty if you need to. However, as with other benefit options, your monthly check will be permanently reduced for withdrawing benefits before FRA.

If your spouse began taking benefits before they died, you can't delay withdrawing your survivor's benefits to get delayed credits. The Social Security Administration maintains you can only get as much from a survivor's benefit as your deceased spouse might have received had they lived.[49]

---

[48] Social Security Administration. "Retirement Planner: If You Are Divorced." https://www.ssa.gov/planners/retire/divspouse.html

[49] Social Security Administration. "Social Security Benefit Amounts For The Surviving Spouse By Year Of Birth" https://www.ssa.gov/planners/survivors/survivorchartred.html

Taxes, Taxes, Taxes

With Social Security — as with everything — it is important to consider taxes. It may be surprising, but your Social Security benefits are not tax-free. Despite having been taxed to accrue those benefits in the first place, you may have to pay Uncle Sam income taxes on up to 85 percent of your Social Security.

The Social Security Administration figures these taxes using what they call "the provisional income formula." Your provisional income formula differs from the adjusted gross income you use for your regular income taxes. Instead, to find out how much of your Social Security benefit is taxable, the Social Security Administration calculates it this way:

Provisional Income = Adjusted Gross Income + Nontaxable Interest + ½ of Social Security

See that piece about nontaxable interest? That generally means interest from government bonds and notes. It surprises many people that although you may not pay taxes on those assets, their income will count against you when it comes to Social Security taxation.

Once you have figured out your provisional income (also called "combined income"), you can use the following chart to figure out your Social Security taxes.[50]

---

[50] Social Security Administration. "Benefits Planner: Income Taxes and Your Social Security Benefits" https://www.ssa.gov/planners/taxes.html

Taxes on Social Security

Provisional Income = Adjusted Gross Income + Nontaxable Interest + ½ of Social Security

If you are ___ and your provisional income is___, then …		Uncle Sam will tax ___ of your Social Security
Single	Married, filing jointly	
Less than $25,000	Less than $32,000	0%
$25,000 to $34,000	$32,000 to $44,000	Up to 50%
More than $34,000	More than $44,000	Up to 85%

[51]

This is one more reason why working with financial and tax professionals may benefit you. They can help you look at your entire financial picture to make your overall retirement plan as tax-efficient as possible — including your Social Security benefit.

So, I think Social Security is largely misunderstood because many people have a preconceived notion as to how Social Security should work for them. A couple who are both retired might say they are going to take Social Security at sixty-two or at their full retirement age. However, when we sit down and run through the process to do the planning, we often find that's not the best option.

Let's say one spouse made significantly less than the other, and the couple is adamant that they want to begin taking Social Security once they turn sixty-two. In this case, we might take

---

[51] Social Security Administration. 2023. "Income Taxes And Your Social Security Benefit"
https://www.ssa.gov/benefits/retirement/planner/taxes.html

early retirement for one of them, at sixty-two or prior to their full retirement age, and then we would defer the higher of the two social securities until age seventy to take advantage of the 8 percent annual increase in their benefit. An 8 percent increase for another three years is significant growth in your benefit, and it means that you can offset inflation by growing the Social Security every single year by 8 percent.

If the couple needs some cash flow, or they're adamant that Social Security won't be available in the future, we could start a spouse a little bit earlier. That way, we can grow the Social Security for one spouse for the future, but also start Social Security earlier for the other spouse.

We also look at the spousal benefit. Let's say one was a stay-at-home spouse. That spouse had a working record, but it wasn't nearly as extensive as the other spouse, who was a high earner. If the spouse was home taking care of the children and working, that spouse would be entitled to their working record benefit, whatever that is. Let's say it's $1,000 a month, or 50 percent of the other spouse's benefit. We would decide how best to manage the benefits because we would hate for them to leave that extra money on the table. That happens all the time. Social Security is worth approximately $700,000 to a married couple if it's elected properly, so planning how to use Social Security is a critical part of the planning process. We incorporate a Social Security analysis in every plan, and we show our clients how to maximize their Social Security based on their circumstances and goals.

Working and Social Security: The Earnings Test

If you haven't reached FRA but you started your Social Security benefits and are still working, things get a little hairy.

Because you have started Social Security payments, the Social Security Administration will pay out your benefits (at that reduced rate, of course, because you haven't reached your FRA). Yet, because you are working, the organization must also withhold from your check to add to your benefits, which you are already collecting. See how this complicates matters?

To address the situation, the government has what is called the earnings test. For 2024, you can earn up to $22,320 without it affecting your Social Security check if you're younger than full retirement age. But, for every $2 you earn past that amount, the Social Security Administration will withhold $1. The earnings test loosens in the year of your FRA; if you are reaching FRA in 2024, you can earn up to $59,520 before you run into the earnings test, and the government only withholds $1 for every $3 past that amount.

The month you reach FRA, you are no longer subject to any earnings withholding. For instance, if you are still working and will turn sixty-seven on December 28, 2024, you would only have to worry about the earnings test until December, and then you can ignore it entirely. Keep in mind, the money the government withholds from your Social Security benefits while you are working before FRA will be tacked back onto your benefits check after FRA.[52]

Railroad Retirement Benefits

The Railroad Retirement Act was established in 1934 to address concerns about existing pension programs' ability to provide former railroad employees with old-age benefits.[53] The Act continues to provide benefits to retired and disabled workers, and their dependents, based on their length of employment in the industry. Although there are similarities to Social Security, there are considerable differences, which include payment amounts, eligibility age, and taxation obligations.

---

[52] Social Security Administration. "Receiving Benefits While Working" https://www.ssa.gov/benefits/retirement/planner/whileworking.html
[53] U.S. Railroad Retirement Board. January, 2023. "2023 Agency Overview" https://www.rrb.gov/OurAgency/AgencyOverview

FROM WORK TO WEALTH | 75

Like Social Security, Railroad Retirement Benefits (RRB) are funded from payroll taxes of current employees and employers. Also, both types of benefits are received by retirees as a monthly check. RRBs use the same formula to calculate COLAs as Social Security.

The differences between the two retirement programs are intricate. The average monthly RRB payment is more generous than Social Security because railroad workers pay higher taxes into the program. Another major difference is the age at which railroad workers are eligible to begin collecting benefits: A railroad worker with thirty or more years of service is eligible for full benefits at age sixty without a reduction.

The taxation of RRBs is more complex than Social Security payments. To determine the tax, RRBs are broken down into two components:

- Tier I benefits resemble Social Security, a private pension, or a combination of both
- Tier II benefits are similar to a private pension[54]

The portion of the Tier I benefit equivalent to Social Security is taxed the same way as Social Security benefits, but the portion not equivalent is fully taxable. Regarding the Tier II, a portion is always taxable and subject to ordinary income tax rates.[55]

We offer Social Security planning to all prospective and current clients who go through our planning process. We provide a detailed report called an "Action Plan," which we consider a roadmap to retirement success. One key component to retirement income is figuring out Social Security options and

---

[54] Kurt Woock. Nerdwallet.com. November 30, 2023. "Railroad Retirement Board: What It Is, How It Works"
https://www.nerdwallet.com/article/investing/social-security/what-is-the-railroad-retirement-board

[55] True Tamplin. Financestrategist.com. September 7, 2023. "Is Railroad Retirement Income Taxable?"
https://www.financestrategists.com/retirement-planning/retirement-income-planning/is-railroad-retirement-income-taxable/

the most efficient way to claim a benefit based on the client's individual situation.

CHAPTER 6
401(k)s, IRAs, and Roth IRAs

Have you heard? Today's retirement is not your parents' retirement. You see, back in the day, it was pretty common to work for one company for the vast majority of your career and then retire with a gold watch and a pension.

The gold watch was a symbol of the quality time you had put in at that company, but the pension was more than a symbol. Instead, it was a guarantee — as solid as your employer — that they would repay your hard work with a certain amount of income in your old age. Did you see the caveat there? Your pension's guarantee was *as solid as your employer.* The problem was, what if your employer went under?

Companies that failed couldn't pay their retired employees' pensions, leading to financial challenges for many. Beginning in 1974 with Congress' passage of the Employee Retirement Income Security Act, federal legislation and regulations aimed at protecting retirees were everywhere. One piece of legislation included a relatively obscure section of the Internal Revenue Code, added in 1978 — Section 401(k), to be specific.

IRC section 401, subsection k, created tax advantages for employer-sponsored financial products, even if the main contributor was the employee themselves. Over the years, more employers took note, beginning an age of transition away from pensions and toward 401(k) plans. A 401(k) is a retirement account with certain tax benefits and restrictions on the investments or other financial products inside of it.

Essentially, 401(k)s and their individual retirement account (IRA) counterparts are "wrappers" that provide tax benefits around assets; typically, the assets that compose IRAs and 401(k)s are mutual funds, stock and bond mixes, and money market accounts. However, IRA and 401(k) contents are becoming more diverse these days, with some companies offering different kinds of annuity options within their plans.

Where pensions are defined-*benefit* plans, 401(k)s and IRAs are defined-*contribution* plans. The one-word change outlines the basic difference. Pensions spell out what you can expect to receive from the plan but not necessarily how much money it will take to fund those benefits. With 401(k)s, an employer sets a standard for how much they will contribute (if any), and you can be certain of what you are contributing. Still, there is no outline for what you can expect to receive in return for those contributions.

Modern employment looks very different. A 2022 survey by the Bureau of Labor Statistics determined U.S. workers stayed with their employers for a median of 4.1 years. Workers aged fifty-five to sixty-four had a little more staying power and were most likely to stay with their employer for about ten years.[56] Participation in 401(k) plans appears solid. In a study it conducted, Vanguard reported a record plan participation rate of 83 percent in 2022. Plans with automatic enrollment drew a 93 percent participation rate.[57]

Those statistics make it clear that 401(k) plans have replaced pensions at many companies and, for that matter, a gold watch.

Planning for retirement while having a pension is different from planning for retirement without a pension. If you're fortunate enough to have a pension, you may be ahead of the game. Back in the day, people often worked thirty to forty years

---

[56] Bureau of Labor Statistics. September 22, 2022. "Employee Tenure Summary" https://www.bls.gov/news.release/tenure.nr0.htm
[57] Vanguard. 2023. "How America Saves 2023" https://institutional.vanguard.com/content/dam/inst/iig-transformation/has/2023/pdf/has-insights/how-america-saves-report-2023.pdf

for the same company, received their gold watch. Their pension and Social Security generated income for retirement. Your personal savings were used for additional things like a vacation or two. Workplace pensions in the private sector have gone away for the most part, so if you have a pension, you have a baseline of income that most people don't have.

As I wrote, we have to be mindful of the spousal benefit if you're married. If you have a pension that only pays on your life and you pass away, your spouse gets nothing. If you have a 50 percent spousal benefit, and if you die, your spouse only gets 50 percent of the benefit. When we do our analysis, we make sure we are leveling the income because it's not about *if* you're going to die, it's *when* you're going to die. You can't leave the surviving spouse with no income, so your spousal benefit may dictate how we do some of the planning going forward.

If there is anything to learn from this paradigm shift, it's that you must look out for yourself. Whether you have worked for a company for two years or twenty, you are still the one who has to look out for your own best interests. That holds doubly true when it comes to preparing for retirement. If you are one of the lucky ones who still has a pension, good for you. But for the rest of us, it is likely a 401(k) — or possibly one of its nonprofit- or government-sector counterparts, a 403(b) or 457 plan — is one of your biggest assets for retirement.

Some employers offer incentives to contribute to their company plans, like a company match. On that subject, I have one thing to say: *Do it!* Nothing in life is free, as they say, but a company match on your retirement funds is about as close to free money as it gets. If you can make the minimum to qualify for your company's match at all, go for it.

Now, it's likely that during our working years, we mostly "set and forget" our 401(k) funding. Because it is tax-advantaged, your employer is taking money from your paycheck — before taxes — and putting it into your plan for you. Maybe you were able to pick a selection of investments, or maybe your company only offers one choice of investment in your 401(k). Either way, while you are gainfully employed, your most impactful decision may just be the decision to continue funding your plan in the first place. But when you are ready to retire or move jobs, you have choices to make requiring a little more thought and care.

When you are ready to part ways with your job, you have a few options:
- Leave the money where it is
- Take the cash (and pay income taxes and perhaps a 10 percent additional federal tax if you are younger than age fifty-nine-and-one-half)
- Transfer the money to another employer plan (if the new plan allows)
- Roll the money over into a self-directed IRA

Now, these are just general options. You will have to decide — hopefully with the help of a financial professional — what's right for you. For instance, 401(k)s are typically pretty closely tied to the companies offering them, so when changing jobs, it may not always be possible to transfer a 401(k) to another 401(k). Leaving the money where it is may also be out of the question — some companies have direct cash payout or rollover policies once someone is no longer employed.

Also, remember what we mentioned earlier about how we change jobs more often these days? That means you likely have a 401(k) with your current company, but you may also have a string of retirement accounts trailing you from other jobs.

We often have clients with five or ten different retirement accounts because they've had so many employers during their careers. People tend to know what they have account wise. However, one doctor we worked with proved to an interesting case. We went through the discovery process to build out his action plan, and in the third or fourth meeting, he said:

"We need to start over."

"What did we do wrong?" I asked.

"I forgot about $600,000 that I have in a 401(k) in fund through another hospital."

We had a legitimate chuckle about that because who forgets about $600,000?

That's why we run through our process. People sometimes get consumed by life. When it comes to your retirement income, it's important to be able to pull together *all* your assets, so you can examine what you have and where, and then decide what you will do with it.

Tax-Qualified, Tax-Preferred, Tax-Deferred ... Still TAXED

Financial media often cite IRAs and 401(k)s for their tax benefits. After all, with traditional plans, you put your money in pre-tax, and it hopefully grows for years — even decades — untaxed. That's why these accounts are called "tax-qualified" or "tax-deferred" assets. They aren't *tax-free!* Rarely does Uncle Sam allow business to continue without receiving his piece of the pie, and your retirement assets are no different. If you didn't pay taxes on the front end, you will pay taxes on the money you withdraw from these accounts in retirement. Don't get me wrong: This isn't an inherently good or bad thing; it's just the way it is. It's important to understand, though, for the sake of planning ahead.

In retirement, many people assume they will be in a lower tax bracket. As referenced in the Taxes chapter, for retirees with healthy balances in tax-deferred assets, their retirement marginal tax rate may be the same or even more than their pre-retirement rate. The timing involved with beginning Social Security or in shifting or converting funds out of tax-deferred assets is of strategic concern because of taxes owed on those assets.

Keep in mind, IRAs, 401(k)s, and their alternatives have a few limitations because of their special tax status. For one thing, the IRS sets limits on your contributions to these retirement accounts. If you are contributing to a 401(k) or an equivalent nonprofit or government plan, your annual contribution limit is $23,000 (as of 2024). If you are fifty or older, the IRS allows additional contributions, called "catch-up contributions," of up to $7,500 on top of the regular limit of $23,000. For an IRA, the limit is $7,000, with a catch-up limit of an additional $1,000.[58] Beginning in 2026, catch-up contributions for individuals with income exceeding $145,000 must transfer into a Roth IRA.[59]

Because their tax advantages come from their intended use as retirement income, withdrawing funds from these accounts before you turn fifty-nine-and-one-half can carry stiff penalties. In addition to fees your investment management company might charge, you will have to pay income tax *and* a 10 percent federal tax penalty, with a few exceptions.

The fifty-nine-and-one-half rule for retirement accounts is incredibly important to remember, especially when you're young. Younger workers are often tempted to cash out an IRA from a previous employer and then are surprised to find their checks missing 20 percent of the account value to income taxes, penalty taxes, and account fees.

Many millennials I see in my practice say that while they may be socking money away in their workplace retirement plan, it is often the *only* place they are saving. This could be problematic later because of the fifty-nine-and-one-half rule; what if you have an emergency? It is important to fund your retirement, but you need to have some liquid assets handy as emergency funds. This can help you avoid breaking into your retirement accounts and incurring taxes and penalties because of the fifty-nine-and-one-half rule.

---

[58] Fidelity.com. November 2, 2023. "IRA contribution limits for 2022, 2023, and 2024" https://www.fidelity.com/learning-center/smart-money/ira-contribution-limits

[59] Robert Powell. thestreet.com. "Ask the Hammer: Catch-up Contributions Now Permitted Until 2026" https://www.thestreet.com/retirement-daily/ask-the-hammer/catch-up-contributions-now-permitted-until-2026

RMDs

Remember how we talked about the 401(k) or IRA being a "tax wrapper" for your funds? Well, eventually, Uncle Sam will want a bite of that candy bar. So, when you turn seventy-three, the government requires you to withdraw a portion of your account, which the IRS calculates based on the size of your account and your estimated lifespan. This required minimum distribution (RMD) is the government's insurance it will collect some taxes from your earnings at some point. Because you didn't pay taxes on the front end, you will now pay income taxes on whatever you withdraw — including your RMDs.

Let me reiterate something I pointed out in the Longevity chapter. Beginning at age seventy-three, you are required to withdraw a certain minimum amount every year from your 401(k) or IRA, or else you will face a tax penalty on any RMD monies you should have withdrawn but didn't — and that's on top of income tax. The SECURE Act 2.0 reduced the penalty to 25 percent (from 50 percent). Timely corrections also can reduce the penalty to 10 percent.[60]

Even after you begin RMDs, you can still continue contributing to your 401(k) or IRAs if you are still employed, which can affect the whole discussion on RMDs and possible tax considerations. The SECURE Act 2.0 raised the RMD age to seventy-three from seventy-two. In addition, the latest legislation stipulates the RMD age will increase to seventy-five for those turning seventy-four after December 31, 2032.[61]

If you don't need income from your retirement accounts, RMDs can seem like more of a tax burden than an income boon. While some people prefer to reinvest their RMDs, this comes with the possibility of additional taxation: You'll pay income taxes on your RMDs and then potential capital gains taxes on

---

[60] Jim Probasco. Investopedia.com. January 6, 2023. "SECURE 2.0 Act of 2022" https://www.investopedia.com/secure-2-0-definition-5225115
[61] Ibid.

the growth of your investments. If you are legacy-minded, there are other ways to use RMDs, many of which have tax benefits.

SECURE 2.0 Act provisions
In addition to changes imposed for RMD ages, Secure Act 2.0 also expanded access to retirement savings using different methods. Provisions in the legislation go into effect at different times, ranging from 2023-25.
- Beginning January 2, 2024, plan participants can access up to $1,000 (once a year) from retirement savings for emergency, personal, or family expenses without paying a 10 percent early-withdrawal penalty.
- Beginning January 2, 2024, employees can establish a Roth emergency savings account of up to $2,500 per participant.
- Beginning January 2, 2024, domestic abuse survivors can withdraw the lesser of $10,000 or 50 percent of their retirement account without penalty.[62]
- Beginning January 1, 2023, victims of a qualified, federally declared disaster can withdraw up to $22,000 from their retirement account without penalty.[63]

Permanent Life Insurance
One way to turn those pesky RMDs into a legacy is through permanent life insurance. Assuming you need the death benefit coverage and can qualify for it medically, if properly structured, these products can pass on a sizeable death benefit to your beneficiaries — tax-free — as part of your general legacy plan.

---

[62] Betterment.com. January 12, 2023. "SECURE Act 2.0: Signed into Law" https://www.betterment.com/work/resources/secure-act-2

[63] Charlie Pastor. Motley Fool. February 16, 2023. "Law Opens New Doors for Penalty-Free Retirement Account Distributions" www.fool.com/the-ascent/buying-stocks/articles/law-opens-new-doors-for-penalty-free-retirement-account-distributions.

ILIT

Another way to use RMDs toward your legacy is to work with an estate planning attorney to create an irrevocable life insurance trust (ILIT). This is basically a permanent life insurance policy placed within a trust. Because the trust is irrevocable, you would relinquish control of it, but unlike with just a permanent life insurance policy, your death benefit won't count toward your taxable estate.

Annuities

Because annuities can be tax-deferred, using all or a portion of your RMDs to fund an annuity contract can be one way to further delay taxation while guaranteeing your income payments (either to you or your loved ones) later. Of course, this assumes you don't need the RMD income during your retirement.

Qualified Charitable Distributions

If you are charity-minded, you may use your RMDs toward a charitable organization instead of using them for income. You must do this directly from your retirement account (you can't take the RMD check and *then* pay the charity) for your withdrawals to be qualified charitable distributions (QCDs), but this is one way of realizing some of the benefits of a charitable legacy during your own lifetime. You will not need to pay taxes on your QCDs, and they won't count toward your annual charitable tax deduction limit, plus you'll be able to see how the organization you are supporting uses your donations. You should consult a financial professional on how to correctly make a QCD.

We use software to help us with RMDs from 401(k)s and IRAs. Sometimes, a distribution model on paper doesn't work in actuality. The software walks us through a process with an understanding of the income tax implications. We have to more or less guess what taxes will be in the future because when you're planning for an RMD you are looking at whether to pull money out early and take the distribution so that you can start to draw down on those qualified accounts.

If you don't, and you keep kicking the can down the road and deferring, you are growing that asset until you are seventy-three and have to withdraw. If the market conditions are good, you're sixty-seven, and you have six years of decent returns until you're seventy-three, you could potentially be making your issue worse by growing those assets because you'll have to take more money out, which is taxable. That could push you up into a higher tax bracket. So, we help you manage the tax brackets and the cash flow. It might make sense to start making withdrawals at age sixty-seven versus waiting until seventy-three.

Roth IRA

Since the Taxpayer Relief Act of 1997, there has been a different kind of retirement account — or "tax wrapper" — available to the public: the Roth. Roth IRAs and Roth 401(k)s each differ from their traditional counterparts in one big way: You pay your taxes on the front end. Once your post-tax money is in the Roth account, as long as you follow the rules and limitations of that account, your distributions are truly tax-free. You won't pay income tax when you take withdrawals, so in turn, you don't have to worry about RMDs. However, Roth accounts have the same limitations as traditional 401(k)s and IRAs when it comes to withdrawing money before age fifty-nine-and-one-half, with the added stipulation that the account must have been open for at least five years for the account holder to make withdrawals.

RMDs and Roth conversions go somewhat hand in hand. When looking at RMDs, we are also looking at whether there's an opportunity for a Roth conversion. Some clients like them in theory, but then when they realize they'll have to pay upfront taxes for the conversion, it seems less attractive. So, we explain that if you're sixty-seven, there's an amount you could convert to stop you crossing over the line to the next tax bracket. It might be $50,000 or more, but if you do those conversions for the next six years, assuming your income stays fairly stable and the tax law doesn't change too much, we can see the net benefit of the conversion.

Taking Charge

As mentioned earlier, the 401(k) and IRA have largely replaced pensions, but they aren't an equal trade.

Pensions are employer-funded; the money feeding into them is money that wouldn't ever show up on your pay stub. Because 401(k)s are self-funded, you must actively and consciously save. This distinction has made a difference when it comes to funding retirement. Fidelity Investments published a study detailing the average 401(k) balance for a person aged fifty-five to sixty-four is $189,800, but the median likely tells the full story. The median 401(k) balance for a person aged fifty-five to sixty-four is $56,450. Those figures reflect Fidelity accounts from the third quarter of 2022.[64]

There can be many reasons why people underfund their retirement plans, like being overwhelmed by investment choices or taking withdrawals from IRAs when they leave an employer. Still, the reason at the top of the list seems to be this: People simply aren't participating to begin with.

So, whether you use a 401(k) with an employer or an IRA alternative with a private company separate from your workplace, the most important retirement savings decision you can make is to sock away your money somewhere in the first place.

---

[64] Arielle O'Shea. Nerd Wallet. December 22, 2022. "The Average 401(k) Balance by Age" https://www.nerdwallet.com/article/investing/the-average-401k-balance-by-age

CHAPTER 7
Annuities

In my practice, I offer my clients a variety of products — from securities to insurance — designed to help them work toward their financial goals. You may be wondering: Why single out a single product in this book?

Well, while most of my clients have a pretty good understanding of business and finance, I sometimes find those who have the impression magic must be involved. Some people assume there is a magic finance wand we can wave to change years' worth of savings into a strategy for retirement income. But it's not as easy as a goose laying golden eggs or the Fairy Godmother turning a pumpkin into a coach!

Finances aren't magic; it takes lots of hard work and, typically, several financial products and strategies to pull together a complete retirement plan. Of all the financial products I work with, it seems people find none more mysterious than annuities. And, if I may say, even some of those who recognize the word "annuity" have a limited understanding of the product. So, in the interest of demystifying annuities, let me tell you a little about what an annuity is.

In general, insurance is a financial hedge against risk. Car owners buy auto insurance to protect their finances in case they injure someone or someone injures them. Homeowners have house insurance to protect their finances in case of a fire, flood, or another disaster. People have life insurance to protect their finances in case of untimely death. Almost juxtaposed to life insurance, people have annuities in case of a long life; annuities can give you financial protection by providing consistent and reliable income payments.

The basic premise of an annuity is you, the annuitant, pay an insurance company some amount in exchange for their contractual guarantee they will pay you income for a certain time period. How that company pays you, for how long, and how much they offer are all determined by the annuity contract you enter into with the insurance company.

Ways You Get Paid

There are several ways for an annuity contract to provide income: annuitization, income riders, partial surrenders, and settlement options for heirs.

Annuitization

When someone "annuitizes" a contract, it is the point where they turn on the income stream. Once a contract has been annuitized, there is no going back. With annuities, if the policyholder lives longer than the insurance company planned, the insurance company is still obligated to pay them, even if the payments end up being way more than the contract's actual value.

If, however, the policyholder dies an untimely death, depending on the contract type, the insurance company may keep anything left of the money that funded the annuity. Nothing would be paid out to the contract holder's survivors. You see where that could make some people balk? Now, modern annuities rarely rely on annuitization for the income portion of the contract, and instead have so many bells and whistles that the old concept of annuitization seems outdated, but because this is still an option, it's important to at least understand the basic concept.

Riders

Speaking of bells and whistles, let's talk about riders. Modern annuities have a lot of different options these days, many in the form of riders you can add to your contract for a fee. The fee typically amounts to 0.1 percent to 1 percent of the contract value per year.[65] Each rider has its particulars, and the types of riders available will vary by the type of annuity contract purchased, but I'll just briefly outline some of these little extras:

- Lifetime income rider: Contract guarantees you an enhanced or flexible income for life
- Death benefit rider: Contract pays an enhanced death benefit to your beneficiaries, even if you have annuitized
- Return of premium rider: Guarantees you (or your beneficiaries) will at least receive back the premium value of the annuity
- Long-term care rider: Provides a certain amount, sometimes as much as twice the normal income benefit amount for a period of time to help pay for long-term care if the contract holder is moved to a nursing home or assisted living situation

This isn't an extensive look, and usually the riders have fancier names based on the issuing company, like "Lorem Ipsum Insurance Company Income Preferred Bonus Fixed Index Annuity rider," but I just wanted to show you what some of the general options are in layperson's terms.

Partial Surrender

Most annuities offer a free withdrawal provision that is often referred to as a partial surrender. An annuity contract typically allows for an annual withdrawal of up to 10 percent, typically,

---

[65] Shawn Plummer. The Annuity Expert. 2024. "Annuity Fees: What You Need To Know" https://www.annuityexpertadvice.com/types-of-annuities/annuity-fees/

of the account value or of the premium originally paid. The option to make this withdrawal, typically without penalty, can be used as a tool to help with your income planning strategies. Keep in mind, the withdrawal is subject to income taxes, and an additional 10 percent IRS penalty if you're under age fifty-nine-and-one-half.

This percentage can be accessed during the surrender period and can be a sound strategy, especially for a client who does not require a regular influx of income provided by a rider. After the surrender value period, the holder of the annuity can access the annuity without losing control of the account value.

I find the partial surrender strategy to often be effective for my clients, particularly if they do not need regular income generated through the use of a rider. A partial surrender allows for the annuity holder to just take out funds when a need arises.

Settlement Options

While any value of an annuity left to beneficiaries upon the annuity holder's death is fairly self-explanatory, there is a point worth raising. Heirs have different settlement options they can consider, including opportunities for lump sums, periodic payments, or specific payouts.

Specific payouts are often based on tax considerations involving a beneficiary or multiple beneficiaries. As an advanced tax planning measure, I have clients who have addressed tax implications with their heirs regarding the most advantageous method for arranging a settlement option that eases any tax burden on the beneficiary.

Types of Annuities

Annuities break down into four basic types: immediate, variable, fixed, and fixed index.

Immediate

Immediate annuities primarily rely on annuitization to provide income. You give the insurance company a lump sum up front, and your payments begin immediately. Once you begin receiving income payments, the transaction is irreversible, and you no longer have access to your money in a lump sum. When you die, any remaining contract value is typically forfeited to the insurance company.

All other annuity contract types are "deferred" contracts, meaning you fund your policy as a lump sum or over a period of years. You give it the opportunity to grow over time — sometimes years, sometimes decades.

Variable

A variable annuity is an insurance contract as well as a security product. It's sold by insurance companies, but only through someone who is also registered to sell security products. With a variable annuity contract, the insurance company invests your premiums in sub-accounts that are tied to the stock market.

This makes it a bit different from the other annuity contract types because it is the only contract where your money is subject to losses because of market declines. Your contract value has a greater opportunity to grow, but it also stands to lose. Additionally, your contract's value will be subject to the underlying investment's fees and limitations — including capital gains taxes, management fees, etc. Once it is time for you to receive income from the contract, the insurance company will pay you a certain income, locked in at whatever your contract's value was.[66]

---

[66] A variable annuity is sold by prospectus. Carefully read the prospectus before purchasing a variable annuity."

Fixed

A traditional fixed annuity is pretty straightforward. You purchase a contract with a guaranteed interest rate, and when you are ready, the insurance company will make regular income payments to you at whatever payout rate your contract guarantees. Those payments will continue for the rest of your life and, if you choose, for the remainder of your spouse's life.

Fixed annuities don't typically offer significant upside potential, but many people like them for their guarantees and predictability. After all, if your Aunt May lives to be ninety-five, knowing she has a paycheck later in life can be her mental and financial safety net. Unlike variable annuities, which are subject to market risk and might be up one year and down the next, you can easily calculate the value of your fixed annuity over your lifetime.

Fixed Index

To recap, variable annuities take on more risk to offer more possibilities to grow. Fixed annuities have less potential growth, but they protect your principal. In the last couple of decades, many insurance companies have retooled their product line to offer fixed index annuities, which are sort of midway between variable and fixed annuities on that risk/reward spectrum. Fixed indexed annuities offer greater growth potential than traditional fixed annuities but less than variable annuities. Like traditional fixed annuities, however, fixed index annuities are protected from downside market losses.

Fixed index annuities earn interest that is tied to an external market index, meaning that instead of your contract value growing at a set interest rate like a traditional fixed annuity, it has the potential to grow within a range. Your contract's value is credited interest based on the performance of an external market index like the S&P 500® while never being invested in the market itself. You can't invest in the S&P 500® directly, but based on when you contract credits interest to your account (e.g., 1 years — point-to-point, 2 years — point-to-point, etc.), your annuity has the potential to earn interest based on the chosen index's performance. The interest is subject to limits set by the company (such as caps, spreads, and participation rates).

For instance, if your contract caps your interest at 5 percent, then in a year that the S&P 500® gains 3 percent, your annuity value increases 3 percent. If the S&P 500® gains 35 percent, your annuity value gets a 5 percent interest bump. But since your money isn't actually invested in the market with a fixed index annuity, if the market nosedives (such as happened during 2000, 2008, 2020, and 2022, anyone?), you won't see any increase in your contract value. Insurance carriers charge Mortality & Expense fees (M&E fees) and may charge additional administrative fees to maintain the insurance policy contract that can lower your contract value. Conversely, there will also be no decrease in your contract value, no matter how badly the market performs. As long as you follow the terms of the contract, you won't lose any of the interest you were credited in previous years.

So, what if the S&P 500® shows a market loss of 30 percent? Your contract value isn't going anywhere unless you purchased an optional rider. This charge will still come out of your annuity value each year, along with M&E fees and possibly administrative fees). For those who are more interested in protection than significant growth potential, fixed index annuities can be an attractive option. When the stock market has a long period of positive performance, a fixed index annuity can enjoy conservative growth. And during stretches where the stock market is erratic and stock values across the board take significant losses? Fixed index annuities won't lose anything due to the stock market volatility.

I'd estimate that 20 to 30 percent of the investible assets that we receive in-house go into a fixed-income annuity or some type of annuity product. Fixed index annuities replicate a personal pension. Let's say you are a policeman, fireman, school teacher, or government employee, your parents may have had a pension. You might love the idea of getting a paycheck in retirement every January 1, February 1, or March 1 like your parents did. We can replicate that by trading some assets that you currently have into a fixed index annuity.

An annuity could have an income rider that allows your money to grow in a controlled environment. There is a guaranteed floor, which is typically zero. If the market takes a downturn, you'll get zero, and then there is a cap that doesn't change. If the cap is 6 percent, your money will be working from 0 to 6 percent based on the performance of the underlying indices. So, there's an opportunity for growth on that money that would probably outperform a bond. It's a guaranteed income stream regardless of the performance, and it provides more certainty around income so that the wild swings of the market don't derail your plan.

Other Things to Know About Annuities

We just explained the four kinds of annuity contracts available, but all of them have some commonalities as annuities.

For all annuities, the contractual guarantees are only as strong as the insurance company that sells the product, which makes it important to thoroughly check the credit ratings of any company whose products you are considering.

Annuities are tax-deferred, meaning you don't have to pay taxes on interest earnings each year as the contract value grows. Instead, you will pay ordinary income taxes on your withdrawals. These are meant to be long-term products, so like other tax-deferred or tax-advantaged products, if you begin taking withdrawals from your contract before age fifty-nine-and-one-half, you may also have to pay a 10 percent federal tax penalty. Also, while annuities are generally considered illiquid, some contracts allow you to withdraw up to 10 percent of your contract value every year. Withdraw any more, however, and you could incur additional surrender penalties.

Keep in mind, your withdrawals will deplete the accumulated cash value, death benefit, and possibly the rider values of your contract.

Many of our clients participate in some type of annuity. People want certainty as they get closer to retirement. And why would you keep all of your assets market-based? If we can take 20 to 30 percent of your overall investible assets and put them into a product that will allow for some guaranteed income, that brings a sense of confidence.

As I mentioned, I've worked with Wall Street bankers and a couple of larger firms that have had a rough go in the last few years. Many of my clients had the opportunity to take a lump sum on their pension, and we looked to see if an annuity could outperform their pension benefits if they chose that route. Let's say their pension benefit would be $1,000 a month, we take the lump sum and shop that lump sum in the open market to see if we can beat the income of $1,000 a month with an annuity. Whether we are successful depends on the prevailing interest rates.

Annuities aren't for everyone, but it's important to understand them before saying "yea" or "nay" on whether they fit into your plan; otherwise, you're not operating with complete information, wouldn't you agree? Regardless, you should talk to a financial professional who can help you understand annuities, dissect your particular financial needs, and show you whether an annuity is appropriate for your retirement income plan.

CHAPTER 8

Estate and Legacy Planning Strategies

In my practice, I devote a significant portion of my time to matters of estate and legacy planning strategies. That doesn't mean drawing up wills or trusts or putting together powers of attorney or anything like that. After all, I'm not an estate planning attorney. But I am a financial professional, and what part of the "estate" isn't affected by money matters?

I've included this chapter because I have seen many people do estate planning wrong. Clients, or clients' families, have come in after experiencing a death in the family and have found themselves in the middle of probate, high taxes, or a discovery of something unforeseen (often long-term care) draining the estate.

I have also seen people do estate planning right: clients or families who visit my office to talk about legacies and ways to make them last, and adult children who have room to grieve without an added burden of unintended costs or stress from a family fractured because of inadequate planning.

I'll share some of these stories here. However, I'm not going to give you specific advice, since everyone's situation is unique. I only want to give you some things to think about and to underscore the importance of planning ahead.

I have two strategic partners for the legal aspects of estate planning: one small and one larger firm. The smaller firm is geared towards the client with fewer investible assets or a lower net worth. For clients with assets in multiple states or real estate assets, the larger firm is a better fit.

They have locations in fifteen or sixteen different states and have more sophisticated planning techniques for more complex situations and business owners looking for business continuation planning. If you are looking to make a will or complete a power of attorney health care directive, our smaller partner offers reasonable rates. I believe that less is more, and we don't need to overcomplicate the planning process unnecessarily, so we only refer clients for what they need.

You Can't Take It With You

When it comes to legacy and estate planning strategies, the most important thing is to *do it*. I have heard people from clients to celebrities (rap artist Snoop Dogg comes to mind) say they aren't interested in what happens to their assets when they die because they'll be dead. That's certainly one way to look at it. But I think that's a very selfish way to go about things. We all have people and causes we care about, and those who care about us. Even if the people we love don't *need* what we leave behind, they can still be fined or legally tied up in the probate process or burial costs if we don't plan for those. And that's not even considering what happens if you become incapacitated at some point while you are still alive. Having a plan in place can greatly help reduce the stress of those responsibilities on your loved ones; it's just a loving thing to do.

Documents

There are a few documents that lay the groundwork of legacy planning. You've probably heard of all or most of them, but I'd like to review what they are and how people commonly use them. These are all things you should talk about with an estate planning attorney to establish your legacy.

Powers of Attorney

A power of attorney, or POA, is a document giving someone the authority to act on your behalf and in your best interests. These come in handy in situations where you cannot be present (think of a vacation where you get stuck in Canada), or for durable powers of attorney (DPOA), even when you are incapacitated (think in a coma or coping with dementia).

It is important to have powers of attorney in place and to appoint someone you trust to act on your behalf in these matters. Have you ever heard of someone who was incapacitated after a car accident, whether from head trauma or being in a coma for weeks — sometimes months? Do you think their bills stopped coming due during that time? I like my phone company and my bank, but neither one is about to put a moratorium on sending me bills — particularly not for an extended or interminable period. A power of attorney would have the authority to pay your mortgage or cancel your cable while you are unable.

You can have multiple POAs and require them to act jointly.
What this looks like: Do you think two heads are better than one? One man, Chris, significantly relied on his two sons' opinions for both his business and personal matters. He appointed both sons as joint POA, requiring both their signoffs for his medical and financial matters.

You can have multiple POAs who can act independently.
What this looks like: Irene had three children with whom she routinely stayed. They lived in different areas of the country, which she thought was an advantage; one month she might be hiking out West, the next she could enjoy the newest off-Broadway production, and the next she could soak up some Southern sun. She named her three children as independently

authorized POAs, so if something happened, no matter where she was, the child closest could step in to act on her behalf.

You can have POAs who have different responsibilities.

What this looks like: Although Luke's friend Claire, a nurse, was his go-to and POA for health-related issues, financial matters usually made her nervous, so he appointed his good neighbor, Matt, as his POA in all of his financial and legal matters.

In addition to POAs, it may be helpful to have an advanced medical directive. This is a document where you have pre-decided what choices you would make about different health scenarios. An advanced medical directive can help ease the burden for your medical POA and loved ones, particularly when it comes to end-of-life care.

I have a client named Joel, who worked for a large Fortune 500 company. Joel had a significant amount of money in his 401(k). Joel developed brain cancer. Before he received treatment, we transferred the power of attorney, especially the financial power of attorney, to his wife Jeannie, so that we could make the proper decisions for his 401(k) and plan holistically for their retirement. Thank God we did. Sadly, Joel's chemo and radiation treatment took a significant toll on his mental capacity. He was cancer free, but he wasn't able to make any real decisions.

The power of attorney meant that his wife and his family could make the right recommendations prior to him undergoing treatment, which set them up for some retirement success. Unfortunately, Jeannie was diagnosed with cancer also, and she actually passed away. Joel's still alive and doing well in retirement because the necessary planning was done. The power of attorney was changed to his oldest daughter after Jeanie passed away.

Wills

Perhaps the most basic document of legacy planning, a will is a legal document wherein you outline your wishes for your estate. When it comes to your estate after your death, having a will is the foundation of your legacy. Without one, your loved ones are left behind to guess what you would have wanted, and the court will likely split your assets according to the state's probate laws. As far as anyone knows, maybe that's exactly what you wanted, right? Because even if you told your nephew he could have your car he's been driving, if it's not in writing, it still might go to the brother, sister, son, or daughter to whom you aren't speaking.

However, it may not be enough just to have a will. Even with a will, your assets will be subject to probate. Probate is what we call the state's process for determining a will's validity. A judge will go through your will to question if it conflicts with state law, if it is the most up-to-date document, if you were mentally competent at the time it was in order, etc. For some, this is a quick, easily resolved process. For others particularly if someone steps forward to contest the will, it may take years to settle, all the while subjecting the assets to court costs and attorney's fees.

One other undesirable piece of the probate process is that it is a public process. That means anyone can go to the courthouse, ask for copies of the case, and discover your assets. They can also see who is slated to receive what and who is disputing.

We try to structure our planning to help avoid the probate process because of the stress it causes the family. It limits the infighting that can occur in families, the government getting more than it should, or funds being tied up in a process that drags on. If you want to be discreet about your wealth, we don't want probate to air out publicly. So, we try to eliminate any problems by doing that work early.

It's also important to remember beneficiary designations trump wills. So, that large life insurance policy? What if, when you bought it fifteen years ago, you wrote your ex-husband's name on the beneficiary line? Even if you stipulate otherwise in your will, the company that holds your policy will pay out to your ex-spouse. Or how about the thousands of dollars in your IRA you dedicated to the children thirty years ago, but one of your children was killed in a car accident, leaving his wife and two toddlers behind? That IRA is going to transfer to your remaining children, with nothing for your daughter-in-law and grandchildren.

That may paint a grim portrait, but I can't underscore enough the importance of working with a skilled estate planning attorney to keep your will and beneficiary designations up to date as your life changes.

The loved ones of Hollywood actor Philip Seymour Hoffman suffered when he died leaving a $35 million estate. He was survived by his girlfriend, Mimi, and their three children, ages ten, seven, and five. Hoffman did not want "trust fund kids" so he used a will to leave his $35 million estate to his girlfriend, who was to provide for their children. However, because of bad estate planning, the estate owed taxes of around $12 million. If Philip had married Mimi, his family would have saved approximately $12 million and paid no estate tax whatsoever.[67]

Trusts

Another piece of legacy planning to consider is trusts.

A trust is set up through an attorney who appoints and authorizes a trusted party or trustee(s) to administer the trust (e.g., make decisions, manage the assets in the trust, distribute funds from the trust, etc.) according to the provisions of the trust agreement.

Many people are skeptical of trusts because they assume trusts are only appropriate for the fabulously wealthy. A simple

---

[67] John M. Goralker. Kiplinger. "Philip Seymour Hoffman's $12 Million Estate Planning Mistake."
https://www.kiplinger.com/article/retirement/t021-c032-s014-philip-seymour-hoffman-s-estate-planning-mistake.html

trust will likely cost more than $1,000 if prepared by an estate planning attorney, and fees can be higher for couples.[68] But a trust can help you avoid both the expense and publicity of probate, provide a more immediate transfer of wealth, avoid some taxes, and provide you greater control over your legacy.

For instance, if you want to set aside some funds for a grandchild's college education, you can make it a requirement that they enroll in classes before your trust will dispense any funds. Like a will, beneficiary designations will override your trust conditions, so you still should be keeping your beneficiary designations on insurance policies, investment account (e.g., 401(k)s, IRAs), and other assets up to date.

Like any financial or legal consideration, there are many options these days beyond the simple "yes or no" question of whether to have a trust. For one thing, you will need to consider if you want your trust to be revocable (you can change the terms while you are alive) or irrevocable (can't be changed; you are no longer the "owner" of the contents).

A brief note here about irrevocable trusts: Although they have significant and greater tax benefits, they are still subject to a Medicaid look-back period. If you transfer your assets into an irrevocable trust in an attempt to shelter them from a Medicaid spend-down, you will be ineligible for Medicaid coverage of long-term care for five years. However, an irrevocable trust can avoid both probate and estate taxes, and it can even help protect assets from legal judgments against you.

Another thing to remember when it comes to trusts, in general, is that even if you have set up a trust, you must remember to fund it. In my twenty years' work, I've had numerous clients come to me assuming they have helped protect their assets with a trust. When we talk about taxes and

---

[68] Rickie Houston. smartasset.com. August 31, 2022. "How Much Does It Cost to Set Up a Trust? https://smartasset.com/estate-planning/how-much-does-it-cost-to-set-up-a-trust

other pieces of their legacy, it turns out they never retitled any assets or changed any paperwork on the assets they wanted in the trust. So, please remember, a trust is just a bunch of fancy legal papers if you haven't followed through on retitling your assets.

Taxes

Although charitable contributions, trusts, and other tax-efficient strategies can reduce your tax bill, it's unlikely your estate will be passed on entirely tax-free. Yet, when it comes to building a legacy that can last for generations, taxes can be one of the heaviest drains on the impact of your hard work.

For 2024, the federal estate exemption was $13.61 million per individual and $27.22 million for a married couple, with estates facing up to a 40 percent tax rate after that.[69] Currently, the new estate limits are set to increase with inflation until January 1, 2026, when they will "sunset" back to the inflation-adjusted 2017 limits.[70] And that's not taking into account the various state regulations and taxes regarding estate and inheritance transfers.

Another tax concern "frequent flyer": retirement accounts.

Your IRA or 401(k) can be a source of tax issues when you pass away. For one thing, taking funds from a sizeable account can trigger a large tax bill. However, if you leave the assets in the account, there are still required minimum distributions (RMDs), which will take effect even after you die. If you pass the account to your spouse, they can keep taking your RMDs as is, or your spouse can retitle the account in their name and receive RMDs based on their life expectancy. Remember, if you don't take your RMDs, the IRS will take up to 25 percent of your

---

[69] Kiplinger.com. Katelyn Washington. November 15, 2023. "Estate Tax Exemption Amount Increases for 2024"
https://www.kiplinger.com/taxes/estate-tax-exemption-amount-increases
[70] IRS.gov. December 20, 2022. "What's New — Estate and Gift Tax"
https://www.irs.gov/businesses/small-businesses-self-employed/whats-new-estate-and-gift-tax

required distribution (10 percent if corrections are made in a timely fashion). You will still have to pay income taxes whenever you withdraw that money. Provisions in the original SECURE Act require anyone who inherits your IRA, with few exceptions (your spouse, a beneficiary less than ten years younger, or a disabled adult child, to name a few), will need to empty the account within ten years of your death.

Also — and this is a pretty big also — check with an estate planning attorney if you are considering putting your IRA or 401(k) in a trust. An improperly titled beneficiary form for the IRA could mean the difference of thousands of dollars in taxes. This is just one more reason to work with a financial professional, one who can strategically partner with an estate planning attorney and also, a tax advisory, to diligently check your decisions.

CHAPTER 9

Women Retire Too

I help women, and families from all walks of life on their journey to and through retirement. However, we want to address the female demographic specifically. Why? To be perfectly blunt, women are more likely to deal with poverty than men when they reach retirement.

The overall poverty rate for women slightly exceeds the rate for men, but among those seventy-five years and older, 13.51 percent of women live at the poverty rate compared to 8.82 percent of men.[71]

The topics, products, and strategies I cover elsewhere in this book are meant to help address retirement concerns for men *and* women, but the dire statistic above is a reminder that much of traditional planning is geared toward men. Male careers, male lifespans, male health care. The bottom line is women's career paths often look much different than men's, so why would their retirement planning look the same?

Women often embrace different roles and values than men as workers, wives, mothers, and daughters. They are more apt to take on roles as caretakers, thus women are likely to spend portions of their lives making hard shifts between family and careers. Time out of the workforce means less income accumulation for investments and retirement. Also, non-

---

[71] statistica.com. 2023. "Poverty rate in the United States in 2021, by age and gender" https://www.statista.com/statistics/233154/us-poverty-rate-by-gender/

working years count as zeroes when calculating Social Security benefits. Women who strongly value family and community tend to focus on lifetime gifting and legacy funding, sometimes to the detriment of their own lifestyles.

These unique choices, challenges, and hurdles make a solid case that women deserve special consideration from financial professionals. The argument is further promoted by the fact that 69 percent of men in the U.S. age sixty-five and older happen to be married, compared to 47 percent of women in that age classification.[72] Single women don't have the opportunity to capitalize on the resource pooling and potential economies of scale accompanying a marriage or partnership.

Generally speaking, I don't think anyone should be treated differently. However, it has been my experience that many advisors tend to prioritize planning for the men, and women-specific concerns are sometimes brushed aside. I spend a lot of time asking questions. If a woman is single or divorced, we'll have a focused conversation on what they want. If it's a married couple, I'll ask the wife a lot of questions to find out what they want because two spouses will never be in one hundred percent agreement.

Sometimes one of the spouses will talk for the other, but we really need to understand how both spouses feel about the market and risk factors to find a balance so that both feel secure in the plan.

Be Informed

With all the couples I've seen, there is almost always an "alpha" when it comes to finances. It isn't always men. For many of my coupled clients, the wife is the alpha who keeps the books and budgets and knows where all of the family's assets are, down to the penny. Yet, statistically, among baby boomers, it is usually

---

[72] Administration for Community Living. November 30, 2022. "Profile of Older Americans" https://acl.gov/aging-and-disability-in-america/data-and-research/profile-older-americans

a man who runs the books. But as time goes on, it looks like the ratio of male to female financial alphas is evening out, based on my experience speaking with couples.

Because most of the baby boomer alphas are men, there is an all too familiar scene in many financial offices across the country: A woman comes into an appointment carrying a sack full of unopened envelopes. Often through tears, she sits across the desk from a financial professional and apologizes her way through a conversation about what financial products she owns and where her income is coming from. She is recently widowed and was sure her spouse was taking care of the finances, but now she doesn't know where all their assets are kept, and her confidence in her financial outlook has wavered after walking through funeral expenses and realizing she's down to one income.

Often, she may be financially "okay." Yet, the uncertainty can be wearying, particularly when the family is already reeling from a loss. While this scenario sometimes plays out with men, in my experience, it's more likely to be a woman in that chair across from my desk. Although the practice has been leveling more and more in recent decades, for centuries Western traditions held money management down as being "a guy thing." But it doesn't have to be this way. This all-too-common scenario can be wiped away with just a little preparation.

Talk to Your Spouse/ Work with a Financial Professional

While there are many factors affecting women's financial preparation for and situation in retirement, I cannot emphasize enough that the decision to be informed, to be a part of the conversation, and to be aware of what is going on with your finances is absolutely paramount to a confident retirement.

The breakdown regarding couples and finances seems to happen because of a lack of communication The breakdown often seems to stem from no one other than the financial alpha knowing how much the family has and where. In the end, it doesn't matter who handles the money; it's about all parties being informed of what's going on financially.

There are a lot of ways to open the conversation about money. One woman, Ann, started a conversation with her husband the financial alpha, by sitting down and saying, "Teach me how to be a widow." Perhaps that sounds grim, but it was to the point, and it spurred what she said was a very fruitful conversation. Couples sometimes have their first real conversation about money, assets, and their retirement income approach in our office. The important thing about having these conversations isn't where, it's when. The best "when" is as soon as possible.

Ann told me that after they got the conversation rolling, she and her husband spent a day — just one part of an otherwise dull weekend — going through everything she might need to know. They spent the better part of two decades together after that. When he died and she was widowed, she said the "widowhood" talk had made a huge difference. She knew who to call to talk through their retirement plan and where to call for the insurance policy.

She said the benefit of the weekend exercise they engaged in some twenty years earlier couldn't have been more apparent than when she ultimately accompanied a recently widowed friend to a financial appointment. Her friend was emotional the whole time, afraid she would run out of money any day. The financial professional ultimately showed the friend that she was financially in good shape, but not before the friend had already spent months worried that each check would exhaust her bank account. That's no way to live after losing a loved one. It was preventable had her deceased spouse and financial professional included her in a conversation about "widowhood."

Spouse-Specific Options

One area where it might be especially important to be on the same page between spouses is when it comes to financial products or services that have spousal options. A few that come to mind are pensions and Social Security, although life insurance and annuity policies also have the potential to affect both spouses.

With pensions, taking the worker's life-only option is somewhat attractive. After all, the monthly payment is bigger. However, you and your spouse should discuss your options. When we're talking about both of you as opposed to just one lifespan, there is an increased likelihood at least one of you will live a long, long time. This means the monthly payout will be less, but it also helps ensure that no matter which spouse outlives the other, no one will have to suffer the loss of a needed pension paycheck in their later retirement years.

While we covered Social Security options in a different chapter, I think some of the spousal information bears repeating. Particularly, if you worked exclusively inside the home for a significant number of years, you may want to talk about taking your Social Security benefits based on your spouse's work history. After all, Social Security is based on your thirty-five highest-earning years.

Things to remember about the spousal benefits:[73]

- Your benefit will be calculated as a percentage (up to 50 percent) of your spouse's earned monthly benefit at their full retirement age (or FRA).
- For you to begin receiving a spousal benefit, your spouse must have already filed for their benefits, and you must be at least sixty-two.
- You can qualify for a full half of your spouse's benefits if you wait until you reach FRA to file.
- Beginning your benefits earlier than your FRA will reduce your monthly check, but waiting to file until after FRA will not increase your benefits.

---

[73] Social Security Administration. "Retirement Planner: Benefits For You As A Spouse" https://www.ssa.gov/planners/retire/applying6.html

For divorcees:[74]
- You may qualify for an ex-spousal benefit if ...
    a. You were married for a decade or more
    b. **and** you are at least sixty-two
    c. **and** you have been divorced for at least two years
    d. **and** you are currently unmarried
    e. **and** your ex-spouse is sixty-two (qualifies to begin taking Social Security)
- Your ex-spouse does not need to have filed for you to file on their benefit.
- Similar to spousal benefits, you can qualify for up to half of your ex-spouse's benefits if you wait to file until your FRA.
- If your ex-spouse dies, you may file to receive a widow/widower benefit on their Social Security record as long as you are at least age sixty and fulfill all the other requirements on the preceding alphabetized list.
    a. This will not affect the benefits of your ex-spouse's current spouse

For widow's (or widower's, for that matter) benefits:[75]
- You may qualify to receive as much as your deceased spouse would have received if ...
    a. You were married for at least nine months before their death
    b. **or** you would qualify for a divorced spousal benefit (if you were divorced and your ex-spouse dies)
    c. **and** you are at least sixty
    d. **and** you did not/have not remarried before age sixty

---

[74] Social Security Administration. "Retirement Planner: If You Are Divorced" https://www.ssa.gov/planners/retire/divspouse.html
[75] Social Security Administration. "Survivors Planner: If You Are The Worker's Widow Or Widower" https://www.ssa.gov/planners/survivors/ifyou.html#h2

- You may earn delayed credits on your spouse's benefit *if* your spouse hadn't already filed for benefits when they died.
- Other rules may apply to you if you are disabled or are caring for a deceased spouse's dependent or disabled child.

Longevity

On average, women live longer than men. Most stats put average female longevity at about two years more than men. But averages are tricky things. An April 2022 report by the World Economic Forum listed the eight oldest people in the world to all be women. They ranged in age from 114 years old to 118 and included two Americans.[76]

It's an exciting time to be a woman, as their potential life paths are vast and less subject to judgment than probably at any point in history. Want to stay at home and raise children? Wonderful! Get a PhD in Astrophysics and work for NASA? Fantastic! Do a combination of both? It's happening! On one hand, women all have unique personalities, goals, ambitions, and passions. However, they share biological and instinctual traits that, in general, give rise to longer lives. And, on that note, the trend for women to live longer presents longstanding financial ramifications.

Joint life planning is essential between two spouses. The income should be leveled so that regardless of who lives the longest, if the husband lives to a hundred or the wife lives to a hundred, we need to make sure that the income stays the same. That's the general premise around planning. We can't leave somebody starving in retirement after their significant other passes away.

---

[76] Martin Armstrong. World Economic Forum. April 29, 2022. "How old are the world's oldest people?"
https://www.weforum.org/agenda/2022/04/the-oldest-people-in-the-world/

Simply Needing More Money in Retirement

Living longer in retirement means needing more money. Period. Barring a huge lottery win or some crazy stock market action, the date you retire is likely the point at which you have the most money you will ever have. Not to put too grim a spin on it, but the problem with longevity is the further you get away from that date, the further your dollars have to stretch. If you only planned to live to a nice eighty-something but instead live to a nice 100-something, that is *two decades* you will need to account for monetarily.

To put this in perspective, let's say you like to drink coffee as an everyday splurge. Not accounting for inflation or leap years, a $4 cup-a-day habit is $29,200 over a two-decade span. Now, think of all the things you like to do that cost money. Add those up for twenty years of unanticipated costs. I think you'll see what I mean.

More Health Care Needs

In addition to the cost of living for a longer lifespan is the fact that aging — plain and simple — means more health care, and more health care means more money. Women are survivors. They suffer from the morbidity-mortality paradox, which states women suffer more non-fatal illnesses throughout their lifetime than men, who experience fewer illnesses but higher mortality.

Women have been found to seek treatment more often when not feeling well and emphasize staying healthy when older, according to studies. Survival, I believe, is on the side of the woman. However, surviving things (such as cancer) also means more checkups later in life.

A statistical concern for women involves the prospect of long-term care. Long-term care for women lasts 3.7 years on average compared to 2.2 years for men.[77]

Widowhood

Not only do women typically live longer than their same-age male counterparts, but they also stand a greater chance of living alone as they age. Some divorce, separate, or never marry. Among those age sixty-five and over, 33 percent of women live alone compared to 20 percent of men.[78]

I don't write this to scare people; rather, I think it's fundamentally important to prepare my female clients for something that may be a startling *but very likely* scenario. At some point, most women will have to handle their financial situations on their own. A little preparation can go a long way, and having a basic understanding of your household finances and the "who, what, where, and how much" of your family's assets is incredibly useful. It can prevent a tragic situation from being more traumatic.

In my opinion, the financial services industry sometimes underserves women in these situations. Some financial professionals tend to alienate women, even when their spouses are alive. I've heard several stories of women who sat through meeting after meeting without their financial professional ever addressing a single question to them.

In our firm, when we work with couples, we work hard to make sure our retirement income strategies work for *both* people. No matter who the financial alpha is, it's important for everyone affected by a retirement strategy to understand it.

---

[77] Lindsay Modglin. singlecare.com. February 15, 2022. "Long-term care statistics 2022" https://www.singlecare.com/blog/news/long-term-care-statistics/

[78] statistica.com. November 23, 2022. "Share of senior households living alone in the United States 2020, by gender" https://www.statista.com/statistics/912400/senior-households-living-alone-usa/

For my clients, our process involves planning for the unfortunate loss of a spouse, so if it happens, the plan remains effective and in place. My approach is to spend time with the widow and provide them reassurance that the plan is working. We might refresh the plan to reinforce things and to show how the decisions we made ten or fifteen years ago are now taking shape. The main thing is that I stay in the trenches and hold their hand during a difficult time. Showing them that they have the means to continue on with their retirement goals relieves some of the pressures.

You can use a robo-advisor or a Fidelity advisor that you talk to over the phone, but that person doesn't know you, and they'll probably never meet you. They might be your advisor for six months and then move on. But I think most people want to be heard and seen. They want to know that you're going to be there when they need you. It's when these types of life events occur and we get in the trenches with the client that our value becomes clear.

Taxes

One of the often-unexpected aspects of widowhood is the tax bill. Many women continue similar lifestyles to the ones they shared with their spouses. This, in turn, means continuing to have a similar need for income. However, after the death of a spouse, their taxes will be calculated based on a single filer's income table, which is much less forgiving than the couple's tax rates. With proper planning, your financial professional and tax advisor may be able to help you take the sting out of your new tax status.

Caregiving

In addition to the financial burden created by caregiving responsibilities, many women often devote many hours each day to duties such as housekeeping and looking after loved ones. So then, when can women find the time to focus long and hard on financial matters?

Unfortunately, the impact and hardships created by traditional roles for women typically do not account for Social Security benefit losses or the losses of health care benefits and retirement savings. This also doesn't account for maternity care, mothers who homeschool, or women who leave the workforce to care for their children in any way.

I don't repeat these statistics to scare you. In America, about 53 million serve as unpaid caregivers and spend roughly $7,000 annually on out-of-pocket caregiving costs.[79] Yet, I think the emotional value of the care many women provide their elderly relatives or neighbors cannot be quantified. So, to be clear, this shouldn't be taken as a "why not to provide caregiving" spiel. Instead, it should be seen as a call for "why to *prepare* for caregiving" or "how to lessen the financial and emotional burden of caregiving."

Funding Your Own Retirement

For these reasons, women should be prepared to fund more of their own retirements. There are several savings options and products, including the spousal IRA. They are like a typical IRA except used by a person who's married. The working spouse must earn at least as much money as is contributed into the IRA.[80] This is something to consider, particularly for families where one spouse has dropped out of the workforce to care for a relative. Also, if you find yourself in a caregiving role, talk to your employer's human resources department. Some companies have paid leave, special circumstances, or sick leave

---

[79] TheScanFoundation.org. November 10, 2022. "Family caregivers are unsung heroes" https://www.thescanfoundation.org/the-buzz/family-caregivers-are-unsung-heroes.

[80] Andrea Coombes. Nerdwallet.com. November 2, 2023. "Spousal IRA: What It Is, How to Open One" https://www.nerdwallet.com/article/investing/spousal-ira-what-it-is-and-why-you-should-open-one

options you could qualify for, making it easier to cope and helping you stay longer in the workforce.

Saving Money

Women likely need more money to fund their retirements. But this doesn't have to be a significant burden. Often, women are better at saving, while usually taking less risk in their portfolios. One source identified many ways for how women are crushing this retirement component.[81]

- In a 2021 analysis of five million Fidelity customers over a ten-year period, women's investment rates of return outperformed men by .04 percent.
- Wells Fargo found that women take approximately 82 percent of the risk men take.
- Meghan Railey, co-founder and CEO of Optas Capital wrote, "While we have found that male clients tend to eagerly invest in the latest asset class everyone is talking about, like cryptocurrency, female clients do not generally jump on the shiny bandwagon."
- Women do a better job buying and holding quality stocks and avoid impulsive decisions. Staying invested for the long haul is often cited as the most effective investing strategy.
- Women remain calm and are less likely to liquidate their retirement accounts during market volatility.
- Lastly, Vanguard found women are less active investors, logging on to their accounts half as often as men and trading 40 percent less frequently.

With all the hurdles to retirement that are unique to women, it's exciting they inherently have an advantage when it comes to saving. This gives me reason to believe as women get more

---

[81] Lyle Daly. The Motley Fool. September 26, 2023. "Investing for Women: What You Should Know"
https://www.fool.com/research/women-in-investing-research/

involved in their finances, families will continue to become more confident about retirement.

CHAPTER 10

Indexed Universal Life Insurance

My clients are not typically gamblers. A day at the races is more likely to give them nightmares than it is to make them eager with dollar signs in their eyes. Many would rather work with at least some guarantees than primarily with stocks and risk-based products, so of course, that often means turning more toward life insurance, and often to a product called indexed universal life insurance — also commonly referred to as fixed indexed universal life insurance.

If you've never heard of that before, I'm not surprised. This life insurance product isn't appropriate for everyone, but I want to take a second to talk about it because, for the right person, it can be a significant product in their financial arsenal.

Insurance: The Basics

If you haven't been casting around in the life insurance pond much, then let's take a second to cover the basics. During our working lives, it's likely we have some kind of basic term life policy, either privately or through our employers. Term life insurance means an individual is protected for a certain period of time — usually ten to thirty years. It typically correlates to a certain amount of wages (if it's an employer's plan) or a coverage amount chosen by the individual (if it's a person's private insurance).

At its most basic, term insurance provides funds for our loved ones and can be used for a number of purposes, including covering funeral expenses or something of that nature. Oftentimes, people will take out more than this. For instance, families with a stay-at-home parent sometimes purchase policies based on the working parent's life to cover years of income, plus the mortgage, etc. Your premium for a term life policy will be based on things like your coverage limit, your age, your health, and the term of the policy.

The older you are, the more likely it is you have health events or other issues that could make it more difficult to obtain term life insurance and the more expensive it is. Some consumers may see this as a disadvantage of term life insurance because they pay into a policy for twenty years. Then, it reaches its "endowment" — the end of the contract term — and there are no additional benefits.

Permanent Insurance

Aside from the basic term life policies many wage-earners hold, insurance companies also have permanent policies, also sometimes referred to as "cash value insurance." With a permanent insurance contract, your policy will typically remain in force as long as you continue to keep it funded (there is an exception for whole life policies, which we'll get to later). A permanent insurance contract has two pieces: the death benefit and cash value accumulation.

Both are spelled out in your contract. As these products gained recognition, people began to realize the products had significant advantages when it came to taxes. I don't want to get too technical, but it really is the technical details that make these policies valuable to their owners. That bit about tax advantages makes permanent life insurance policies attractive to consumers. Not only do they receive an income-tax-free death benefit for their beneficiaries, but they may also be able to borrow against their policy, income-tax-free, if they end up needing the money.

For example, let's say Emma purchases a life insurance policy when she's thirty. She hates the idea of not having anything to show for her premiums over ten to twenty years, so she decides to use a permanent policy. Then, when she's close to fifty, her brother finds himself in dire straits. Emma wants to help, and she's been a diligent saver. The catch is most of her money is in products like her 401(k) or an annuity. These may be products appropriate for her needs, but her circumstances have just changed, and she's looking for ways to help her sibling without incurring significant tax penalties.

But wait … she has that permanent life insurance policy! She can borrow any accumulated cash value against her policy, free of income taxes. So, let's say she borrows a few thousand dollars from her policy. She doesn't have to pay taxes on any of it. She can pay it back into her policy at any time. Then, let's say Emma dies before she "settles up" her policy (or pays back that loan). As long as she continues to pay premium payments or otherwise keeps her policy adequately funded until she dies, then her beneficiaries will still receive a death benefit minus the policy loan.

Are you with me so far? Here are the central themes on properly structured permanent life insurance policies: tax-free death benefit and income-tax-free withdrawals through policy loans are available as long as the premiums continue to be paid, and a minimum rate of cash value accumulation is guaranteed by the strength of the insurer.

Now, let's dive a little deeper into the two basic categories of permanent insurance on the market: whole life policies and universal life policies.

Whole Life Insurance

With whole life, an actuary in a back office has calculated what a person your age with your intended death benefit coverage, your health history, your potential lifespan — and other minutia — should pay for a premium rate. Depending on how the insurer calculates rate tables, your whole life policy will "endow" at a certain age — ninety, 100, 120, etc. — so there is the risk you could outlive the policy. The death benefit would pay out to you instead of your beneficiaries, which may create unplanned tax consequences.

Nonetheless, to qualify for your whole life policy, you will complete a medical questionnaire and possibly a paramedical exam, and based on that information, an underwriter will place you in one of these actuarial categories to determine your premium rate. One benefit of whole life insurance is the insurance company will credit a certain amount back into the policy's cash value based on your contract's guaranteed rate. Some insurance companies may also pay a dividend back to policyholders at the company's discretion.

Take Emma from the preceding example, and let's consider the scenario if her permanent insurance policy was a whole life policy. When she first purchased the contract, the insurance agent would have been able to tell her what her locked-in premium rate would be. She would pay the same amount, year after year, to keep her contract in force. And she could also calculate her policy's minimum cash value to the penny.

Universal Life Insurance

If whole life is the basic permanent life insurance policy, universal is the souped-up model. It has eight speeds, comes in many colors, and has more options, which means it might take some extra time and research to be thoroughly understood. But this means if it's right for you, it can be even more customizable and fine-tuned to your specific needs.

The major differences:
- Flexible premium
- Increasing policy costs

Let's start with those increasing policy costs. Basically, the internal cost to the insurance company of maintaining your policy will increase over time, like a term insurance policy. Remember how whole life policies have those actuaries at the insurer's office calculating all of that and then determining a set rate for you to pay to cover it all? Well, with universal life, that's part of the flexible premium part. You can decide to pay a premium that will cover your future policy expenses, or you can decide to pay a premium that barely covers your current policy expenses, depending on your circumstances.

That is where these policies have gotten a bad rap in the past. If you purchase a policy and only ever pay the minimum premium required, your policy could lose value to the point that your premium no longer covers your policy's expenses, and then the policy would lapse. That's also why it's incredibly important to work with a financial professional you trust. This financial professional should shoot straight about whether this kind of product would be appropriate for you and make sure you fully understand all the details.

To return to our example of Emma, though, here's how a well-set-up universal life insurance policy could work: Emma, ever the diligent saver, would have paid well over the minimum premium every month. Every time she got a raise or payroll increase, she increased the amount of premium she paid into her policy. With the policy's contractual rate of interest, she had a substantial amount of cash value accumulated in the policy. That way, when she decided to borrow money against the policy to help her brother, she could even afford to decrease her monthly payments for a time, until she was back in a better financial position.

Indexing

Now to the main event: *indexed* universal life insurance (IUL). Like any permanent insurance, an IUL policy will remain in force as long as you continue to pay sufficient premiums, and you can borrow against your policy's cash value, income-tax-free. At their core, IUL policies are universal life insurance policies with flexible premiums. So, how are they different?

If you skim back through some of the other policy details, I covered the ability to withdraw the cash value of your policy without paying income taxes, even on the accumulation. Because of the index part of IULs, that accumulating cash value has the potential to accumulate more. An index is a tool that measures the movement of the market, like the S&P 500® or the Dow Jones Industrial Average. You can't invest directly in an index. It's just a sort of ruler.

With an IUL policy, your cash accumulation interest credits are based on an index, with what is called a "floor" and a "cap" or other limits such as a spread or participation rate. If the market does well, each year your policy can be credited interest on the cash accumulation based on whatever your policy's index is, subject to the cap, spread, or participation rate. If the market has a bad year and the index shows negative gains, your account still gets credited, whatever your contract floor is.

So, for example, let's say your contract cap is 12.5 percent and the floor is 0 percent. If the market returns 20 percent, your contract value gets a 12.5 percent interest credit. The next year, the S&P 500® returns a negative 26 percent. The insurance company won't credit your policy anything, but you also won't see your policy value slip because of that negative performance (although M&E fees and administrative fees will still be deducted from your policy). So, your policy won't lose value because of poor market conditions, but you can still stand to realize interest credits due to changes in an index.

Another opportunity IUL policies present is for a policyholder to overfund the policy cash value in the first five or ten years and then, potentially, not have to pay any more money into the policy, letting the cash accumulation self-fund the policy. However, when overfunding an IUL policy, it is important to understand the policy may become a modified endowment contract (or MEC) if premium payments exceed certain amounts specified under the Internal Revenue Code.

This can happen if a policy has been funded too quickly in its early years. For MECs, distributions during the life of the insured (including loans) are fully taxable as income to the extent there is a gain in the policy over the amount of net premiums paid. An additional 10 percent federal income tax may apply for withdrawals made before age fifty-nine-and-one-half.

Another opportunity IUL presents is for a policyholder to overfund the policy cash value in the first five or ten years and then, potentially, not have to pay any more money into the policy, letting the cash accumulation self-fund the policy. However, when overfunding an IUL policy, it is important to understand the policy may become a modified endowment contract (or MEC) if premium payments exceed certain amounts specified under the Internal Revenue Code. This can happen if a policy has been funded too quickly in its early years. For MECs, distributions during the life of the insured (including loans) are fully taxable as income to the extent there is a gain in the policy over the amount of net premiums paid. An additional 10 percent federal income tax may apply for withdrawals made before age fifty-nine-and-one-half.

So, back to our friend, Emma. If her permanent life insurance policy was an IUL, what might that have looked like? Emma saves, paying well over the mandatory minimum of her IUL policy. Let's assume the market does well for decades. Her policy accumulates a significant cash value. At some point, she stops paying as much in premium, or maybe she stops paying any premium from her own pocket at all because her policy has enough cash value to pay for its own expenses with the insurance company. Then, when her brother needs help, there is enough cash value stored in the policy.

It's important to note that making withdrawals or taking policy loans from a policy may have an adverse effect. You may want to talk to your financial professional to re-evaluate your premium payment schedule if you are considering this option.

If you're reeling just a bit, it's understandable. There's a lot going on with these policies. If you don't take the time to understand the basics of how they work, it's entirely possible to fall behind on premium payments and end up with a policy that lapses. Yet, if you understand the terms of your contract and are working with purpose, an IUL policy could be a powerful cog in the greater mechanics of your overall retirement strategy.

You can use an IUL for a few different reasons. There is a death benefit component, and the death benefit can be used for tax planning purposes and estate liquidity. So, when the policyholder dies, it creates liquidity for the beneficiary. The beneficiary could be a spouse, a trust, or the children. Essentially it's instantaneous, so now there's capital, which gives those beneficiaries income tax-free liquidity, but not estate tax-free liquidity.

In this case, an IUL becomes a wealth-creation tool because life insurance has some unique tax benefits. Any funds that go into it are going to grow tax-free and tax-deferred, rather like a Roth IRA. Let's say you commit to using it as an IUL that's been structured for cash value accumulation, and you're going to use it to supplement income in retirement. If it has significant cash value, we can start to draw out some tax-free loans from the policy to supplement your retirement income. At some point, you'll pass away and the death benefit is tax-free for your heirs.

It's a good leverage tool. If you can trade a dollar and get back $5, that's a good move. And if we can do that trade where we're trading a dollar, and we can trade a post-tax dollar to get back tax-free dollars, it's an even better thing.

I think the power of life insurance is misunderstood when you're using it in the context of either wealth creation or estate planning. Most people think life insurance is a cost, but it's sometimes the best love letter you can leave to anybody you care about. Whether that's your spouse, your kids, or your grandkids, it's so impactful to their life, even though you're dead. If you leave your house, your heirs might not want the house. And if there's multiple heirs involved and they don't live in the same state, or one does and others don't, there could be disagreements as to who gets the house and when to sell the house. Life insurance is immediate. It's liquid, simple, and tax free.

CHAPTER 11

Long-Term Care Insurance

Elsewhere in this book, I've outlined the risks longevity poses to your financial health. In fact, you may be tired of hearing it at this point.

Even so, I'd still like to repeat one more time — in case you've forgotten — it's estimated *seven* out of every ten Americans who reach age sixty-five will need long-term care of some kind.[82] Let me ask: If you knew the car you were going to be riding in had a 70 percent chance of having an accident, would you wear your seatbelt?

My mom passed away at age sixty-six from lung and throat cancer, and she was diagnosed about eighteen months prior to that. Towards the end of her fight against cancer, we saw that she wasn't going to win the battle, and she needed care. My sister took a leave of absence, but she's not an aide; she was simply to be there with my mother overnight. My mother needed an aide for most of the day and an RN to come in at least for a couple of hours, sometimes twice a day. This wasn't 24 hour round the clock care, it was care provided at her house by an agency and it cost thousands of dollars per month; at least $5,000 to $7,000. If this type of care is required for both spouses the cost doubles. Although the statistics say 70 percent

---

[82] Lindsay Modglin. singlecare.com. February 15, 2022. "Long-term care statistics 2022" https://www.singlecare.com/blog/news/long-term-care-statistics/

of people over sixty-five will need some type of care, people we see and meet always place themselves in the 30 percent and think it will never happen to them. So, we expose the costs to our clients and at least have a conversation about it. Long-term care is not something that you want to push onto your children.

The bottom line is we need to do a better job of planning for the possibility of long-term care. However, if you think about the current problems plaguing government-run programs such as Social Security, Medicaid, and Medicare, I think it stands to reason we're probably on our own for the time being.

Elsewhere, I covered the various ways of preparing for our own possible long-term care costs, from self-funding to insurance riders. I'd like to take a moment to expand on what is one of the most comprehensive coverage options: long-term care insurance.

LTCI Basics

The long-term care insurance (LTCI) space has had a bit of a shakeup in the past few years. Many insurers stopped offering LTCI, and the policies remaining are often more expensive. In addition, denials of LTCI applications have risen to the point that 38.2 percent of those between the ages of sixty-five and sixty-nine are rejected. The percentage increases to 47 percent for applicants aged seventy to seventy-five.[83]

Yet, on the other side of the coin are the insurers left in the LTCI space. They have experience and policies that have endured. LTCI may be more expensive for individuals, but that's because they can be more expensive for insurers, and overall, long-term care is just plain expensive, period. It's important to understand that LTCI carriers aren't just making money hand-over-fist with these products. Instead, the carriers

---

[83] American Association for Long-Term Care Insurance. 2023. "Nearly Half Of Oldest Long-Term Care Insurance Applicants Denied" https://www.aaltci.org/news/long-term-care-insurance-association-news/applicants-declined

who have stopped selling policies were likely carriers who had unrealistic prices and underperforming policies. According to one report, prices have stabilized yet could still be considered expensive to some.[84]

While many criticize the use-it-or-lose-it nature of LTCI, it is reasonable to consider that homeowner's insurance, car insurance, term life insurance, and many other types of insurance work the same way. Yes, you are paying into a policy in the hopes you may never use it. But if you must use it, it can provide value well beyond the actual dollars you have paid into it. An average of 358,500 experience a structural home fire every year[85] for the 131.43 million households in the United States.[86] I share those numbers because you have *less than a half percent chance* of experiencing a home fire in any given year. However, most of us would still squirm at the thought of not having homeowner's or renter's insurance to cover fire damage. Paradoxically, while LongTermCare.gov cites that those turning sixty-five stand a 70 percent chance of needing long-term care, only 10 percent of Americans have LTCI.[87]

To purchase LTCI, you have to complete an application that includes a medical questionnaire. Depending on your age and the insurance carrier, you may also need to complete a medical exam. If you qualify, then the insurance company will offer you a policy with certain coverage and pricing based in part on your odds of needing long-term care in the future. The younger you are, the more likely you are to qualify — at a rate that is more likely affordable for you.

---

[84] aaltci.org. 2023. "2022 Price Index For Long-Term Care Insurance Released" https://www.aaltci.org/news/long-term-care-insurance-association-news/2022-price-index-for-long-term-care-insurance
[85] thezebra.com. January 31, 2023. "House Fire Statistics" https://www.thezebra.com/resources/research/house-fire-statistics/
[86] Statista. November 22, 2023. "Number of households in the U.S. from 1960 to 2023" https://www.statista.com/statistics/183635/number-of-households-in-the-us
[87] hcgsecure.com. 2022. "Long-Term Care Perceptions & Preparation" https://hcgsecure.com/independent-research/

LTCI premiums count as medical expenses and may potentially be paid with special tax considerations. For instance, if you are eligible to itemize your medical expenses, LTCI premiums can be itemized. Or, alternatively, you can pay premiums with tax-free money in health savings accounts. The amount you can withdraw tax-free for LTCI premiums depends on your age.

If you have an LTCI policy, coverage will typically kick in when you have been medically shown to be unable to perform two or more activities of daily living (ADLs). An ADL is an activity such as bathing, toileting, eating, dressing, grooming, and getting in and out of a bed or chair. These are all things we naturally prefer to do by ourselves. They are markers of our independence and ability to take care of ourselves. Once someone is unable to do some of these things alone, they need long-term help.

So, if you have LTCI, once you reach this point, you will qualify for a daily amount of coverage over a pre-selected time period, depending on the terms of your policy. That money could be used to cover a nursing home stay, in-home care, or community organization care. The benefits will begin after the policy's elimination period, which you choose when you purchase the policy. The elimination period can range from 0 to 180 days, and the shorter the elimination period, the higher the premium.

With LTCI, you can pick and choose facilities or care options according to your standards instead of having the government decide what is best for you.

Long-Term Care Partnership Program

One other significant advantage of LTCI is many plans are eligible for a federal-state government initiative called the Long-Term Care Partnership Program.[88] This program is a

---

[88] American Association for Long-Term Care Insurance. 2023. "Long Term Care Insurance Partnership Plans" http://www.aaltci.org/long-term-

joint effort by the federal government and certain states to help individuals decide to choose LTCI protection. It means if you deplete your LTCI coverage and find yourself in a position of having to spend down your assets to become eligible for Medicaid, part or all of your LTCI coverage limit will extend to your assets. Here's what this might look like "in real life" (using, of course, a completely hypothetical person):

Jennifer chooses an LTCI policy to cover up to three years of nursing home care (a little more than the average long-term care stay) in a semi-private room. After several injuries render her unable to dress or bathe herself, Jennifer moves to Winters Retirement Community. Jennifer is not average. Her policy has paid out more than $250,000 on her behalf, and her policy benefits are now exhausted. This puts her in position for a Medicaid spend down. However, because she purchased a policy her state approved in line with the Long-Term Care Partnership Program, instead of having to spend down her assets to the Medicaid requirement and leaving very little for her family to inherit, she is allowed to set aside $250,000 on top of her state's other spend-down exemptions.[89]

The best approach to long-term care is to have a meaningful conversation about it. By meaningful, I mean a conversation that's authentic and transparent, and then taking some steps, whether that's buying a product for long-term care or allocating money from somewhere else specifically to deal with that issue.

As long as we expose the issue, determine what the potential risks are for you based on your circumstances, your assets and the health history of your family, then we can make a plan that you're comfortable with. Brushing the subject under the carpet and pretending it won't happen is the worst thing to do.

---

care-insurance/learning-center/long-term-care-insurance-partnership-plans.php
[89] American Council On Aging. March 14, 2022. "How Purchasing Long-Term Care Insurance Can Help Medicaid Beneficiaries Protect Their Homes & Assets"
https://www.medicaidplanningassistance.org/partnerships-for-long-term-care/

LTCI — It's Not Just About You

Aside from the partnership program and possible tax advantages of traditional LTCI, I think perhaps one of the most compelling arguments in favor of preparing for the likelihood of long-term care has less to do with our own personal assets and more to do with others.

What do I mean? Well, I hear from lots of people who think it won't matter. "Oh, by the time I reach the point of needing long-term care, I'll be out of my mind. Who cares who takes care of me and how that happens?"

However, like estate planning, long-term care planning isn't solely about us. In fact, I might argue that the most important piece of long-term care planning isn't about you at all. It's about your loved ones. It's about your spouse, your children, or your friends, and how caring for you could impact them if you don't have the necessary resources.

Most caregiving for the elderly happens in people's private homes. One report found that only 11 percent of elderly Americans requiring care services live in a nursing home or assisted living facility.[90] Among other findings:

- Of those surveyed, a mean of nineteen hours a week was provided in care. Among those, about 38 percent had to cut back their hours at their job.
- The average age of an in-home caregiver is forty-nine. Of those providing in-home care, 66 percent are women.

About 1.3 million caregivers are children between the ages of eight and eighteen, with three-fourths of those caring for a parent or grandparent.

Because of its benefits for both the policyholder and their family or caregiver, LTCI can be a valuable asset in any retirement plan.

---

[90] John Hopkins Medicine. 2024. "Being a Caregiver" https://www.hopkinsmedicine.org/health/caregiving/being-a-caregiver

CHAPTER 11

Finding a Financial Professional

Finding a financial professional is a personal endeavor. Allowing someone to examine your finances is like giving them a window into how you manage your life. Most of us are uncomfortable with that type of exposure. The best planners realize that, and are doing what they do to help you live with less stress and worry. Of course, they want to make money, too, but they need to have a passion for making your money work for you and your lifestyle.

I joined this industry because I saw my father's success as a financial advisor in the late 1990s and early 2000s. I was graduating at that time and was trying to figure out what I wanted to do with my life. I had no idea. I thought what my dad did for a living was boring, and I really had no interest. But then he shared with me his success from a financial standpoint, and it was significant. I was blown away. I was young and didn't know anything about money then, but I wanted to know more.

My father was working in a specific space: retirement plans for high-net-worth business owners. That really drew me in because it was a little bit different. He wasn't just a life insurance salesman or an investment advisor. He had a unique twist. So, my father made me an offer that was compelling. I was living in Florida at the time, and he asked me to come back to New Jersey to work for him and learn the ropes from the ground up. I agreed. I did everything in the office: all the grunt work. But it was probably the best thing that could have happened to me because I learned so much. I opened the mail, answered the phone, emailed clients, and helped my father run proposals and create illustrations.

After some time, my father sent me on the road. I visited some of his friends and peers in the industry. Most of them were significantly more well off than my father, and I was excited by their work and lifestyles. One lived in Hollywood and catered to many famous and wealthy clients. My first year was a roller coaster, but I could see it could be a financially rewarding career if I did the right thing for my clients. I admit it. I was bedazzled by the potential to earn a high income.

Most people join a wealth management firm and are expected to produce right away, and if you don't produce, you're out. I didn't have that pressure. If I had, I probably would have failed. I had the luxury of taking my time to learn the industry and decide how I would hone my craft and approach people. It's been a blessing and an amazing experience ever since.

I graduated in business administration. But once I inserted myself into the wealth management industry, I obtained my life and health license and my securities registration.

Once I started helping people with their finances, I realized that it's hard for people to objectively plan for themselves. It's hard to separate your money and your emotions. People make irrational decisions based on their emotions and their circumstances. A financial planner approaches your finances without bias. We'll just shoot it straight. You may or may not like that information at the time, but in the long run, it will be valuable because we are not influenced by the same things as our clients, and we can make more objective decisions. That's when I really started to enjoy what I was doing. I could see the value added to someone like me. It wasn't just about coming up with the next best way to apply your assets. It helped people see things differently and in a way that would change their lives.

I loved the high-net-worth business-owner clients, which was where my father based his business. However, I was drawn to the banking industry. In general, that industry changed a lot just after the financial crisis of 2008 and 2009. There were so many opportunities. The banking industry was so big, and the money they were making was incredible. It provided me with a unique niche. Shortly after the financial crisis, the banks started tightening their belts after new regulations were imposed. Bankers started to lose their jobs, and there was a huge reduction among those employed in the industry. That eliminated some of the opportunities for me. I knew that the bankers would be fine whether I was there or not, so I decided to move into a space where I could be of more value, which was the retirement market.

Find a Good Sounding Board

Unlike my father, who was a specialist in a niche area, I became a generalist in the retirement market. I'm serving the middle class, which is the largest demographic when you consider the baby boomers. Generally speaking, the middle class gets the short end of the stick where financial planning is concerned. Some firms won't accept them as clients because they don't have enough assets, but people from the middle class need the most attention. I built my whole practice around pre-retirees from that demographic. That was my aha moment.

I see myself as a second set of eyes. Things change, but not everybody is interested or willing to have a conversation about finances. My wife is a good example. She doesn't want to have a deep conversation about our finances. She wants to know that we're doing well and that we're doing the right thing. So, we have a more general conversation about numbers and what I want to do with our money, and she's on board for the most part.

Sometimes your spouse isn't the best sounding board for you, and you need to talk to someone who's focused solely on your finances. I am 100 percent focused on a client's goals and objectives the second they engage with us, and that's something that everyone needs. A bit like everyone needs a good therapist.

I have twenty years of experience planning for retirement for clients. I help them figure out how to ensure they have enough money and live a healthy retirement. I help them understand the tax perspective of retirement and the cost of care, whether that's Medicare or long-term care. I help them consider the scenarios and how they play out and what is the cost associated with those scenarios. I do this every single day, and practice gets you closer to perfect.

People often think they are unique, and they can be offended when I tell them that their situation is not unique to me. They tell me their financial worries, and I tell them, "You're going to be fine. I'll prove it to you with the numbers that have worked before."

Having a financial professional that you trust is paramount because when Congress passes a new law, you want to know how it impacts you. My experience is important, but so is staying abreast of industry changes, both inside the wealth-advising world and with regard to regulatory changes and the IRS. We need to provide the most updated advice. Retirement policies don't change on a daily basis, but they do change over time. I don't think there's one person who mapped out retirement at age sixty and then reaches age sixty-five and thinks their plan will stay the same. Many things are out of your control that will affect your retirement; tax law and regulatory changes are two examples. For example, the provisions for the Tax Cut and Jobs Act of 2017 expire at the end of 2025. That's not really on people's radar just yet, but in January 2026, many of our clients will be wondering how their retirement will be affected.

Choose the Relationship, Not the Brand

If you are interviewing financial professionals, and you're trying to figure out who you think is the best fit for you, I recommend not getting caught up in the biggest brand name. They might be leading institutions, but how well can you connect with them on a personal level?

Anybody can use a robo-advisor or a low-cost brokerage like a Charles Schwab, Fidelity, or TD Ameritrade, and they'll get some level of service, but there's not going to be much relationship-building. A planner that works for Fidelity might leave to go somewhere else. That advisor won't take his book with him, and as their client, you'll be shuffled over to another planner who you've never spoken to and now you're starting from scratch. And this could be two years into the process.

Your planner should be there for the long-term; ideally, the rest of your life. They should know your children and your grandchildren and what your values are. If an advisor really wants to do what's best for the client, they need to understand all the dynamics at play. I think people want that connection. They want to feel like they've been heard. They want to make sure that the team they have in place is the right team for them and will be there for the long haul.

I'm in my mid-forties and my lead planner is around 30. Most of our clients are fifty-five to sixty-five. I've found that our clients like the fact that I'm twenty years younger than them. I have enough experience to know what I'm doing, but at the same time, the team is younger. Most people I've talked to don't want an advisor the same age as themselves because when they both get older, there's the issue of diminished capacity. Is someone of the same age going to still be on the cutting edge of the industry? Will they have health issues, and if they do, how will that affect the client?

Do Your Due Diligence

Recommendations for a financial planner are great; however, I would still kick the tires pretty thoroughly. If someone recommended me to a friend or family member, I would want that person to ask me the tough questions. I'm perfectly comfortable answering whatever questions you might throw at me because I want you to know everything about the firm. I want you to know we got into the business, how long we've been in business, how many clients we have, and what our process looks like. I want you to be sure we're the right team for you.

At a bare minimum, before you choose a planner, do your due diligence. Look the person up on FINRA's "Broker Check"[91] to see if they have had any run-ins with the authorities. It happens once in a while, and it's usually fully disclosed. If a broker has had three or four instances of a similar complaint, that's a recurring theme to be wary of.

I tell my client's that I will hold your hand through the retirement planning process. We set the course, and then you're going to tell me how much hand holding you want. You might want to be on your way, and then if you hit a roadblock or some kind of detour, we'll talk about it. Or I'm there to hold your hand the entire way. And some people want that.

When I meet my clients, I want to find out their goals and help them meet them. If I met a client today and they were fifty-seven years old and were thinking about retiring in their early-to-mid sixties. I'd tell them they had a little bit of time. Let's say they wanted to get a good feel for where they are financially, we would run them through our process. In that process, we take their current position and we apply what we call the five risks in retirement to their current situation. The five risks are shown in the graphic below.

---

[91] brokercheck.finra.org. 2024. https://brokercheck.finra.org/

Where We Excel

Comprehensive Planning

- Tax
- Estate
- Health Care
- Income
- Investment Risk & Growth

How do we plan for retirement?

Longevity Risk
('Will I have enough money to live on in retirement?')

Health Risk
('Am I protected against critical illness, injury, and LTC?')

Mortality Risk
('Will my family be ok financially when I'm gone?')

Inflation Risk
('What will my purchasing power be in the future?')

Market Risk
('How can I protect against another 2008 crash?')

For example, the client might be doing great from a potential income generation perspective, but the tax side isn't so great. They might have too much, let's say qualified money, which would be 401(k) that's going to be heavily taxed.

In that case, we might recommend switching gears. If you are fifty-seven and you want to work until you're sixty-five, we have eight years. We could think about funding the Roth component of your 401(k) at work, assuming they have that option, and dial back on some of the qualified money. I would show them exactly why and how that would benefit them. If we catch clients early enough, between the ages of fifty-five and fifty-seven, we can make meaningful changes that help set the course.

Now, if you're sixty-five when we meet you, and you want to retire at age sixty-six, there's not much time to make any major changes, but there are always adjustments that we can make. It's a process of exploring, understanding the data, analyzing that data, applying those risks, and giving that person a retirement roadmap.

The goal is to give the client the confidence to retire. We want to get to the root of their concerns and provide them with an action plan. We want to take some of that weight off their shoulders and allow them to breathe easier knowing that our processes are battle-tested.

Once people see their plans, they feel like they're playing on their own terms. Before, they might have been holding on to their job and feeling like they have to work for three or four more years keeping their head down. But if we do our job, they should be able to go into work thinking, "If this is the day that I've had enough, it's the day I'm going to retire because it's not worth the headache anymore. I've got only one life to live, and I want to enjoy myself."

Acknowledgments

I would like to express my most sincere gratitude to the following individuals and organizations that have supported me throughout my career:

- Advisors Excel: To the entire team at Advisors Excel. You are always looking to find the best industry talent, cutting-edge technology, and most impactful speakers who are always looking to share their keys to success.
- National Life Group: I am thankful for the opportunity previously provided by National Life Group, where I served as a district manager. Their support enabled me to dedicate time and resources to launch and grow a successful and profitable district from scratch.
- Chris Budd: Thank you for your loyalty, commitment, and willingness to learn. Your continued contributions have helped us grow tremendously, and I will be forever grateful.
- Robert Belcuore: Thank you for your invaluable guidance and mentorship. Your energy, passion, and competitive spirit always help push me to a higher level.
- My family and friends: Your love, patience, and understanding sustained me through the highs and lows of this impactful career. I am truly blessed to have such incredible support in my life.

Finally, I extend my heartfelt thanks to all the readers who embark on this journey with me. Your interest and support mean the world to me.

MATTHEW LANG
About the Author

As the managing partner of Wealth Shield Financial, Matt Lang is focused on helping clients work toward their retirement dreams through a well-thought-out strategy for retirement income.

Matt Lang is a financial services industry veteran with over twenty years of experience. He entered the industry shortly after college. Since then, his roles have ranged from back-office support to management, including building and operating a successful independent family insurance agency. He is currently the founder and managing partner of Wealth Shield Financial, a firm he created from the ground up.

From the start of his career, Matt has focused on working with banking executives and business owners. He has extensive experience creating advanced tax planning strategies for high-net-worth individuals and families. He is still passionate about working with these individuals, but has been highly focused on pre-retirees and retirees. Matt feels that middle America is highly underserved and has dedicated his practice to developing retirement strategies to improve retirement success. Matt has used his extensive skills and knowledge to create confidence in his clients so they can live out the retirement they have always wanted and deserve.

Matt holds insurance licenses in California, Connecticut, Florida, Georgia, Indiana, Kansas, Missouri, Montana, New Jersey, New York, North Carolina, Ohio, Pennsylvania, South Carolina, Texas (Insurance License# 1802675), and Virginia. He has earned Series 6 and Series 63 industry designations. Matthew has a B.S. degree in business from Arizona Western College.

Matt is an avid race car fan and race team owner. He currently lives in Bethlehem, Pennsylvania, with his wife, Ashley, and their children: Preston, Addison, and Dillon.

Made in the USA
Middletown, DE
16 April 2024

53055836R00096